AFTER SEBALD

ESSAYS & ILLUMINATIONS

AFTER SEBALD

ESSAYS & ILLUMINATIONS

Gillian Beer

John Coetzee

Tacita Dean

Tess Jaray

Richard Long

Robert Macfarlane

Clive Scott

Will Self

Ali Smith

EDITED BY

JON COOK

FULL CIRCLE EDITIONS

Published in association with UEA

Contents

Introduction / Jon Cook 9

W.G. Sebald / Robert Macfarlane 19

Sebald in the City / Gillian Beer 37

W.G. Sebald / Tacita Dean 50

Loosed in Translation / Ali Smith 71

After Nature / John Coetzee 85

Invisible Jews and Absent Executioners / Will Self 95

LIFEDEATH / Richard Long 117

W.G. Sebald: Enumeration, Photography
and the Hermeneutics of History / Clive Scott 125

Two Pieces / Tess Jaray 143

Select Bibliography 152

Author Biographies 154

Acknowledgements 157

Note on footnotes

The select bibliography at the back of this book gives the publication details of the major works published by W.G. Sebald in their English and German editions. Unless otherwise stated, all the references to Sebald's work in English that follow are to these editions. Footnotes for other publications provide bibliographical details in the footnotes themselves.

Jon Cook

*

Introduction

In the years since his death in 2001, W.G. Sebald's work has not been forgotten. All the books published in his lifetime in English translation remain in print, as does the work published posthumously: *The Natural History of Destruction* in 2003; *Unrecounted* in 2004, the result of a collaboration with the visual artist, Jan Peter Tripp; *Campo Santo* in 2005; a new translation of his selected poems, *Across The Land and The Water*, in 2011; and, in 2013, *A Place in the Country*, a collection of biographical and critical essays. Sebald has passed what is an often brutal test of literary reputation. His death has not been used as an excuse to stop reading him. He is not one of those many authors, like Bulwer Lytton in the 19th century or David Garnett in the 20th, who enjoyed great literary success in their lifetimes only to be forgotten once they died, their memories now only preserved by a few devotees or academic specialists. Sebald, by contrast, both in what he says and in the way he says it, continues to attract a large international readership. And it's not just among readers that his work continues to be a living presence. It may be too early to talk of a 'Sebald tradition', but a number of writers, visual artists and film makers have taken his work as a model and an inspiration. Teju Cole's novel, *Open City*, carries a strong echo of the prose rhythms of *Vertigo* and *Austerlitz;* Edmund de Waal's *The Hare with Amber Eyes* starts with a Sebaldian preoccupation with what has survived the Holocaust; and in 'Patience: After Sebald', the film director, Grant Gee, has taken *The Rings of Saturn* as the basis for a cinematic meditation on what it is that draws us so strongly towards Sebald's imaginative world. The list could be readily extended. It gives some indication of the fact that Sebald's work is not just an achievement in its own right, but a set of potentials waiting to be realized in the work of others as well as in the engaged imaginations of his readers.

When we ask why Sebald's work continues to speak to us a number of answers come readily to mind. He was a writer of deep ethical commitment who felt an obligation to understand, or, at least, return to the difficulty of understanding, some of the most destructive episodes of twentieth century history. The nature of this obligation was at one with a need to remember 'against the grain' of a culture that seemed devoted to ignoring or denying the very things that Sebald wanted to recall. Yet the style of his work is far from didactic. The past seems to flow into his work with a strange hallucinatory quality, one set of recollections embedded in another set of memories, one narrative voice metamorphosing into another, as though consciousness comes into its most vivid imaginative life in a state akin to dreaming. One of the contributors to this volume, Robert Macfarlane, captures something of this quality when he describes finishing a book by Sebald as 'like drifting slowly to a surface from a sea-bed through marine light, stunned and grateful'. The mesmeric quality of his writing, as well as its effort at remembering, is further enhanced by the curious punctuation of his texts by photographs that are only ever partially explained by the flow of language that they interrupt. His books are like rebuses. The combination of words and images in them imply meanings that are both urgent and difficult to translate. There is a similar fluidity and enigmatic quality when we think about Sebald's work in relation to genre. His books seem to move in and out of fiction, autobiography, history, and travelogue. The mood of his work is melancholic, populated by people who, whatever else they might be feeling, are in the grip of an inextinguishable sadness. For some of his readers at least— Susan Sontag amongst them— Sebald's writing recreates the possibility of great literature. There is a stature, a breadth and depth of subject matter, a sense of a heroic undertaking, that, if he had lived, would almost certainly have led to the award of the Nobel Prize.

If responses along these lines summarize some of the characteristics that have established Sebald's reputation, they also carry with them a certain kind of danger. They become ways not so much of reading Sebald as of labeling him and putting him in a box marked 'great writer'. The essays collected in this book, however different in style and approach they may be, are all attempts to save his work from the fate of being taken for granted. They have all been written in the years since his death. Some have been published before; others are published here for the first time. Each registers a vivid trace of what it means to read Sebald intelligently. This means questioning those occasions where his work seems to fail and acknowledging when it might seem oppressive. It also means giving substance to what it means to describe Sebald as a great writer. But not all of the pieces collected here are essays in the conventional sense. The work of the visual artists in this book offers a different range of responses: Richard Long's cryptic memorial; Tacita Dean's adaptation of Sebald's style to her own purposes; or the readings and recollections of Tess Jary, who worked with Sebald on a number of occasions. To set the work of visual artists alongside the work of writers seems an appropriate way of thinking about an author who collected and adapted visual images with the same assiduous care he devoted to the assembly and recreation of written texts.

The implications of this juxtaposition of verbal text and visual image – so marked a feature of Sebald's method – are taken up in a number of essays in this book, especially in Clive Scott's piece on the significance of lists and photographs in Sebald's work. This essay joins with others to illuminate a basic feature of his imaginative method: the idea of authorship as a form of collecting. In this respect his work could be seen as a response to the question raised by another and earlier German writer, Walter Benjamin, who asked, in his aphoristic book *One Way Street*, 'When are we going to able to write books like catalogues?' [1] Benjamin was attracted to the catalogue as a form because it offered possibilities for assembling disparate kinds of material and then thinking about how they might be connected together. And the catalogue was, as well, the form in which things that are thought to be transient or of little value could be preserved and remembered. This way of thinking about writing entered Sebald's imagination. He described the process in his essay on the Swiss writer, Robert Walser:

... I have slowly learned to grasp how everything is connected across space and time, the life of the Prussian writer Kleist with that of a Swiss author who claims to have worked in a brewery in Thun, the echo of a pistol shot across the Wansee with the view from a window at Herisau asylum, Walser's long walks with my own travels, dates of birth with dates of death, happiness with misfortune, natural history and the history of our industries, that of *Heimat* with that of exile. [2]

It is characteristic of Sebald's style that this sentence should take on the form of a catalogue, at once painstaking in its enumeration of examples and also uncanny in the possibilities for connection that it seems to open up. Different moods inform this process: an explorer's pleasure in discovery can mutate into an anxiety about all the connections that wait to be made or that might have been irretrievably lost, and then, a little beyond this anxiety, is the unnerving, vertiginous feeling that there may be an order in the world that can never be known or understood.

If photographic archives were one important source of the activity of collecting that informs Sebald's work so too was the sheer range and miscellaneous character of his reading. His texts are, amongst other things, assemblages of quotations that move from works of philosophy, literature and history to articles in nineteenth century magazines and snippets from radio programmes or train timetables. The English poet, Coleridge, once described himself as a 'library cormorant'. [3] Something similar could be said of Sebald. The catalogue of his personal library runs to over sixty closely printed pages and includes the 1988 Michelin Guide to Great Britain and Ireland as well as the collected works of Shakespeare, Goethe, and Milton. Any or all of these resources, as well as the other libraries he explored, provided the stores out of which his own texts were made. This compositional habit extended to the title of at least one of his books. As Sebald himself notes, his study of the allied bombing of German cities during the Second World War, *The Natural History of Destruction*, borrowed its title from the scientist, Sir Solly Zuckermann, who had intended, just after the war, to write an essay based on his visit to the ruined city of Cologne. He named the essay, 'The Natural History of Destruction', but found himself unable to write it. Some fifty years later Sebald took over what his predecessor had abandoned.

Sebald's books are not in any simple sense a record of this endless activity of collecting, although, as John Coetzee observes, in his essay on Sebald's poem *After Nature*, the narrators in Sebald's stories are often 'engaged in a labour of research'. Rather they are a place where what has been collected can disclose new and often strange patterns. Reading Sebald can be a little like engaging with a special kind of map, one that will reveal previously unimagined connections not just across space but across time as well.

If discovering an archive was as a matter of biographical fact an important element in the composition of many of Sebald's works, it is also true that the idea of the archive, and of other less obviously scholarly forms of information storage like the photograph album or scrapbook, provide models or analogies for the experience of reading Sebald. Like some of his characters, his readers wander through his books as if going through a space that is full of miscellaneous material whose survival or persistence seems pervaded by a sense of how much else has been lost or destroyed. The thought that everything might be connected can be a source of bafflement as well as illumination. The past pervades the present, but not in a way that either Sebald's narrators or his readers can readily understand. If we ordinarily think of memory as the mental activity that recalls the past, in Sebald's work recollection is taken one stage further. Distinctions between past and present experience blur and dissolve so that one seems to overturn or replace the other. Time itself seems transformed or abolished in a way that is described by one of Sebald's characters, Jacques Austerlitz:

> I feel more and more as if time did not exist at all, only various spaces interlocking according to the rules of a higher form of stereometry, between which the living and the dead can move back and forth as they like, and the longer I think about it the more it seems to me that we who are still alive are unreal in the eyes of the dead. [4]

In his essay, 'Absent Jews and Invisible Executioners', Will Self quotes this passage and finds in it a recurrent moment of Sebaldian other-worldliness or transcendence. Yet Austerlitz's vision of time abolished— comparable in many respects to the work of medieval writers like Dante and Chaucer who could imagine a time-bound world from the perspective of eternity— is also something fragile and exposed. Whatever it provides by way of consolation or beauty is embedded in another narrative, the story of Austerlitz's escape from the Holocaust and his subsequent attempts to retrieve a past that has become lost to him. His comments about time having no reality are almost immediately followed by another confession: 'As far back as I can remember, said Austerlitz, I have always felt as if I had no place in reality…'.[5] Similar sentences work like a leitmotif through the novel. They remind us that, in Sebald's work, visionary moments are often also symptoms of loss. They speak of suffering at the same time as they seek to neutralize its effects. They remind us that having visions and being out of your mind are closely allied in Sebald's work and in the traditions it draws upon.

In the 19th century a genre evolved that took as its special subject matter deranged states and enigmatic events. It became known as the 'case study' or 'case history'. The 'case' is a literary and scientific genre in its own right, one practised for example by writers like Edgar Allan Poe and Franz Kafka as well as psychoanalysts like Freud. 'Cases', at least in their literary and psycho-analytic form, deal in a world where nothing can be taken for granted and where anything is possible. Above all, they put in question the idea of the individual as a self-possessed, autonomous being, who has the freedom to choose how to live. Instead, what makes us what we are and makes us do what we do is always likely to exceed our or anyone else's understanding.

While the case history is another of the genres that Sebald inherits, an ethical problem arises that leads him to be extremely cautious about one of its consequences. One sign of this problem is given in the opening section of the first of Sebald's works to be published in English translation, *The Emigrants*. In the second section of the book, Sebald writes about his former teacher, Paul Bereyter, who committed suicide shortly after his seventy fourth birthday by lying down on a railway track and waiting for a train to run over him. As Sebald absorbs this information he finds himself recollecting Bereyter, and, as he recollects, he also starts to imagine him in various situations, living in his flat, tending his garden, and then, taking off his glasses and lying down on the railway track to await his death. This imagining is abruptly checked by two sentences:

> Such endeavours to imagine his life and death did not, as I had to admit, bring me any closer to Paul, except at best for brief, emotional moments of the kind that seemed presumptuous to me. It is in order to avoid this sort of wrongful trespass that I have written down what I know of Paul Bereyter. [6]

These sentences summarize an ethical dilemma that Sebald's work encounters and seeks to resolve: how do you write about the lives of others without trespassing on them and, more particularly, without invading them with the wrong kind of emotion? Can a life be written about and respected at the same time? And is it possible to feel for others without recreating them in the image of our own emotional needs? Does 'knowing' then become a matter of documenting as carefully as possible whatever has been left of a life in records, correspondence, visual images, and the recollections of others?

These same questions resonate throughout the history of the case study. Whether in Freud's work or in the strange melodrama of Edgar Allan Poe, *The Facts in the Case of M. Valdemar*, where a man is hypnotized at the point of death as part of an experiment to see if he can speak after his life has ended, the problem of how another life can be violated, with either the best or the worst of intentions, has been rehearsed over and over again. If Sebald takes from the case study its concern with painstaking documentation, what he tries to overcome is its tendency to treat others as though they were specimens or merely examples of a problem.

The idea that writing about a life might carry the threat of erasing it is one aspect of Sebald's preoccupation with the fact and the consequences of destruction. The word figures in the title of one of his works, *The Natural History of Destruction;* it's there again in the epigraph to the section of *The Emigrants* devoted to Henry Selwyn, 'And the last remnants memory destroys'; and in another epigraph, this time to *The Rings of Saturn*, where we read that Saturn's rings are ' in all likelihood…fragments of a former moon that was too close to the planet and destroyed by its tidal effect'.[7] But destruction doesn't need to be explicitly named to be evoked in Sebald's work. It is there in the apocalyptic visions he discovers in the history of European art or in the landscape and history of cities, as Gillian Beer discovers in her essay 'Sebald in the City'. Starting from the vision at the beginning of *The Rings of Saturn* of the city of Norwich as a 'sea of stone or field of rubble', she discovers something powerful and paradoxical in Sebald's writing about cities. Urban spaces at once 'carry the past and they obliterate it. They are full or people and they void their presence.' We are offered something more than a lament at the consequences of human and natural destruction, if only because Sebald is fascinated by what survives obliteration and the new forms of life that come into being after a catastrophe. We may think that twilight is the pervasive atmosphere of Sebald's work, and that this corresponds to a the melancholic mood of a survivor whose purpose in the world is uncertain. But this is to forget those moments of life and light that can suddenly manifest themselves: the May morning, recalled in *The Emigrants*, when Paul Bereyter teaches his pupils French, that 'bright fresh day we easily grasped what un beau jour meant'; or the moment in *Austerlitz*, one of night time illumination, when the moths 'came flying in as if from nowhere, describing thousands of different arcs and spirals and loops, until like snowflakes they formed a silent storm around the light…'[8]

 A collection of this kind does not have a single purpose, other than to help his readers enjoy and think further about Sebald's work. The writers and artists whose work is gathered here do not share a single view of why Sebald is worth reading. Will Self and Gillian Beer do not have quite the same response to Sebald's preoccupation with human and natural catastrophes. In her essay, which traces what is lost and found, connected and disconnected in Sebald's writing, Ali Smith dissents from the idea that the mood of his work is melancholic. Instead she finds a different emotional inflection, ' an enquiry into despair which produces a tightrope-balanced negotiation between the workings of the mind and being out of your mind'. Robert Macfarlane reflects on what the arguments for and against Sebald can tell us about his work and its reception. Will Self asks whether

English readers, himself included, like Sebald's work because they find in it a moral ascendancy that conforms with an image of the longed-for 'Good German'. Gillian Beer and Ali Smith both find evidence of a strange kind of comedy, one too often overlooked by more solemn interpretations of his significance. John Coetzee writes about a recurrent crisis of melancholy in Sebald's work and reminds us of the significance of his work as a poet. Clive Scott explores the structures of Sebald's style and imagination, its movements between long shot and close up, gravity and levitation. Tacita Dean takes another tack, creating her own version of Sebaldian connectedness. And, in their different ways, Richard Long and Tess Jaray take up another of Sebald's preoccupations: the relation between remembering and commemoration. If these different readings give us the opportunity to gauge the scale of his achievement they suggest something else as well: that Sebald is an author whom we are still learning how to read and one whose works can stand the test not just of time but of different interpretations.

[1] Walter Benjamin, *One Way Street*, trans. Edmund Jephcott and Kingsley Shorter (London, NLB: 1979). p 63.
[2] 'Le Promeneur Solitaire: On Robert Walser', *A Place in the Country*, p149.
[3] Samuel Taylor Coleridge, letter to John Thelwall, 19th November 1796, *The Collected Letters of Samuel Taylor Coleridge*, ed. E.L. Griggs, 6 vols. (Oxford, Clarendon Press: 1956-71). p 260.
[4] *Austerlitz*, p 261.
[5] *Austerlitz*, p 261.
[6] *The Emigrants*, p 29.
[7] *The Emigrants*, np , *The Rings of Saturn*, np
[8] *The Emigrants*, p 38; *Austerlitz*, p 128.

Robert Macfarlane

*

Sebald

If you have never read anything by W. G. Sebald, what should you know about him?

That he died in a car crash in 2001. That, had he lived, it seems likely he would have won the Nobel Prize. That his fame rests chiefly upon four works of what he called 'prose fiction' – *The Emigrants*, *The Rings of Saturn*, *Vertigo* and *Austerlitz* – all published in the eleven years before his death. That he developed a strange, antique literary form which combined memoir, travelogue, anecdote and black-and-white photographs of places (railway stations, seascapes, iron bridges), and found objects (ticket stubs, butterflies, snooker balls, tree roots). That people liken the experience of reading his books to being enchanted, not in the breezily trivial way that writing gets called 'spellbinding' or 'intoxicating' when it is not, but in a way which suggests that something profound, disturbing, pathological has happened to them. That a certain generation of readers will remember where they were and what they were doing when news of his death reached them. That finishing a book by him is like drifting slowly to a surface from a sea-bed through marine light, stunned and grateful.

If you have read anything by W. G. Sebald, what do you know about him?

That the characters in his books are all gnawed to the bone by melancholy. That the narrators of his books are people who eerily resemble, but somehow are not, Sebald himself. That the subjects of his books are the Holocaust, exile, and the morality of memory. That his lovingly decrepit sentences — with their rococo architecture, their clanking anchor-chains of clauses, their elaborate grammar — seem to have been picked up from a different era and set down, unexpectedly, shockingly, in our own. That there are times when, in his technique of fastidious omission, one suspects he has bitten off more than he can eschew. That on occasions he writes badly. That the streets he travels through are often depopulated, that his skies are always grey, and that his stories take place in a heavy dark air, pollinous with thought.

※

Winifred Georg Sebald (1944–2001), who spent most of his working life as a Professor of Modern German Literature at the University of East Anglia, was born and grew up in Wertech im Allgäu, a village in the Bavarian Alps. His father had joined the German army in 1929, and fought for Hitler during the Second World War. He was interned in a French prisoner of war camp, and returned home in 1947 a stranger to his three-year-old son. Sebald recalled that his father never discussed his experiences of the war. Indeed, the rural Germany that Sebald knew as a child was, he remembered, 'that social stratum where the so-called conspiracy of silence was at its most present'. In interview, Sebald told a story about the beginning of his realisation that repression was at work on a massive scale in post-war Germany:

> Until I was 16 or 17, I had heard practically nothing about the history that preceded 1945. Only when we were 17 were we confronted with a documentary film of the opening of the Belsen camp. There it was, and we somehow had to get our minds around it– which of course we didn't. It was in the afternoon, with a football match afterwards. It took years to find out what had happened. In the mid-60s, I could not conceive that these events had happened only a few years back.[1]

Sebald studied German literature at Freiburg University, taking his degree in 1965, and the following year came to Britain; first to Manchester, and then to take up his position at UEA and to live with his wife in an old rectory near Norwich. It was in Manchester, Sebald said, that his next 'phase of realisation' about Germany's amnesia occurred.

> I understood for the first time that these historical events had happened to real people.

> You could grow up in Germany in the postwar years without ever meeting a Jewish person. There were small communities in Frankfurt or Berlin, but in a provincial town in south Germany Jewish people didn't exist. The subsequent realisation was that they had been in all those places, as doctors, cinema ushers, owners of garages, but they had disappeared – or had been disappeared.²

Like J. M. Coetzee, or J. R.R. Tolkien (a writer with whom he shared a comically fogeyish dislike of much of modernity), Sebald established himself as an academic before he attracted attention as a novelist. It was only in his forties that he began writing the books which would make him famous. It was not that Sebald suffered from writer's block. It was just that it took him much of a lifetime to work out a form through which he could approach his chosen subjects – atrocity and remembrance, unexorcised grief – with due diligence and care.

Sebald held the Holocaust Industry largely in contempt, both its anguishedly formal efforts to mourn 'officially' – efforts which he felt turned quickly into self-regarding exercises in the ethics of grief – and in its more sentimental cultural outgrowths, including films such as Schindler's List. 'I knew', he observed, 'that writing about the subject [the Holocaust], particularly for people of German origin, is fraught with dangers and difficulties. Tactless lapses, moral and aesthetic, can easily be committed.' ³

And so he developed his uncanny, piebald, polymorphous mode, which mixed scholarship (the objective, the plan-view) and testimony (the subjective, the ground-view). It is in part this fusion of the aloof and the utterly involved which makes Sebald's work memorable. In his books he was, as John Banville noted, 'doing nothing less than relating the slow suicide of European civilisation'. ⁴ But he was also examining how suffering has, within it, many kinds of perspective: perspectives that can be influenced, diminished and – crucially – exaggerated by history.

Sebald is often acclaimed as a startlingly original writer. Walter Benjamin's dictum about how 'all great works of literature found a genre or dissolve one' ⁵ is often invoked. But he had his influences, and he was happy to admit them. There was Thomas Bernhard, Adalbert Stifter, Stefan Zweig, Yukio Mishima's

'I-novels', Leonid Tsypkin. One of the best things about discovering Sebald is discovering his influences, and reading them as well. There is, however, almost nothing like Sebald in English. Perhaps this is what early German critics meant when they said that he wrote like a ghost: that the voices of an earlier epoch were speaking through him, that his was a style pulled from the rubble of old Europe.

No other writer of recent decades has matched the speed of Sebald's ascent to the pantheon. It occurred in a little over five years. *The Emigrants*, the first book of Sebald's to be published in English, but the second to have been written, appeared in 1996. Then came *The Rings of Saturn* (1998) and *Vertigo* (1999), together forming a loose trilogy. Comparisons were made with Borges, Calvino, Kafka, Proust and Nabokov. Literary opinion-formers on both sides of the Atlantic hoisted Sebald onto their shoulders, including James Wood ('one of the most mysteriously sublime of contemporary writers'),[6] John Banville ('Greatness in literature is still possible'),[7] A. S. Byatt ('One of the most important writers of our time'),[8] and Lynne Sharon Schwartz, who described him shortly after his death as 'the writer we could least afford to lose'.[9] By the time of the publication in 2001 of *Austerlitz*, his masterwork, Sebald was unmistakably a major European author. His death sealed his reputation, and solved the problem of what he would write next.

Three curious things strike me about Sebald's reception. The first is the lack of dissenting voices. The nay-sayers that do exist have barely been heard, their grumblings lost in the bright chorus of praise. Cynthia Ozick wrote a mildly sceptical essay in 1996 called 'The Posthumous Sublime'.[10] Tom Paulin muttered darkly about Sebald's 'postmodern antiquarianism' being 'a million miles away from the real thing'.[11] A long essay by Adam Thirlwell appeared in a little magazine called *Arete*, which made an intermittently persuasive case for Sebald being a tin-pot peddler of kitsch.[12] Otherwise, nothing.

A second curious thing. His reception in Britain and America has been more enthusiastic than his reception in Germany. Hanser Verlag, who published Sebald in hardback in Germany, sold between 4,000 and 5,000 in hardback for the first three books, though *Austerlitz* sold over 25,000 (10,000 following Sebald's death). The books have sold between 15,000 and

20,000 each in paperback. These are modest sales figures. Figures for British and US sales are hard to come by, but they are substantially larger. There is an obvious reason for this discrepancy: that the message Sebald's books carry concerning the consequences of Germany's cultural amnesia doesn't play well with German audiences on a large scale. But there's something else at work, which has to do with the exotic allure of Sebald's Europeanism to an American and British commentariat.

Sebald didn't care much about the fuss that was being made over him, or at least he pretended not to. Allegedly, when Susan Sontag first found herself in the same room as Sebald, during a symposium, she went over to ask if he would like to come for a coffee after the event was over. He said he had to get the next train back to Norwich. Sontag asked if he could get a later train, for they might not get a chance to meet again for several years. He said that he couldn't, that he wanted to get back. When he was profiled by the *New Yorker*, he was asked how he had devised *The Rings of Saturn*. The interviewer clearly expected a heroic creation myth for a book which had been hailed as one of the great works of late-twentieth-century literature. Sebald replied as follows:

> I had this idea of writing a few short pieces for the [...] German papers in order to pay for the extravagance of a fortnight's rambling tour. That was the plan. But then, as you walk along, you find things. I think that's the advantage of walking. It's just one of the reasons I do that a lot. You find things by the wayside or you buy a brochure written by a local historian which is in a tiny little museum somewhere, which you would never find in London. And in that you find odd details that lead you somewhere else.[13]

A third curious aspect to Sebald's popularity is that he is a very difficult writer. Take *The Emigrants*, for instance, which is a biography of four people you will never have heard of – two of them victims of the Nazis, and two of them victims of exile – and whose narrative nooks are chocked full of arcana and esoterica in which you are unlikely to have a pre-existing interest. Or take his last novel, *Austerlitz*, with its densely nested narrators and its 418 unparagraphed pages. Or take *The Rings of Saturn*. I've tried to press this book on people who've never read Sebald. My advocacy usually runs as follows: 'Our narrator, who resembles W. G. Sebald but isn't quite him, traipses mournfully around East Anglia, ruminating on ruination, transience, futility, depression, and historical catastrophes. Along the way he tells us disconnected stories about Swinburne, Edward Fitzgerald, the deforestation of Britain, the contemporary poet and translator Michael Hamburger, a drowned town, and the herring trade. I can't recommend it highly enough'. My interlocutors tend to nod too much, their eyes glazing over by the time I reach the word 'Anglia'.

What I should say is something like this: '*The Rings of Saturn* has no truck with sentimentality, none of the contemptible eagerness for reader sympathy which mars so much fiction today. Its story, if it can be said to possess one, occurs in dreamily slow motion, and is recounted in a register which is bewitchingly alienating to the reader. It's a weird, strabismic take on the English landscape as something brimming with tragic history, a book which reveals Britain's borders to have been far more porous to the atrocities of twentieth-century European history than we might think, and that its buildings and its landscapes have absorbed and archived the conflicts of the last hundred years. It's a book which, astonishingly, finds depth in the flattest, most apparently unsprung region of all England, in a landscape so flat that you could fax it.' But somehow I never quite get all that out.

I don't especially want to defend Sebald, or to attack him, though I'm interested in the reasons why people might want to do either. What I want to do is firstly to say something about what people have found extraordinary in Sebald's work, and then to say something about what feels wrong to me at times in his writing. Neither is an easy task. The extreme resistance of Sebald's prose to interpretation is one of the reasons why he has already attracted so many interpreters. His writing operates as a mood, rather than as a set of propositions, and as such it is often its own best expression.

Certainly, Sebald's work incites inarticulacy. People are moved to speak of their experiences of reading him, but often find they are unable to say exactly what happened. His writing disturbs the hive of the imagination. It sets the mind softly ringing for weeks and months afterwards. When I talk with people about Sebald, they often use the language of hypnosis, or narcosis, to describe the effect he had on them. They use words like 'compulsive', 'magic', 'mesmeric'; words which testify to a sense of a brain-magic having been worked, to readers having been forced to think in ways beyond their volition or their control. Others use the language of abduction – 'spellbound', 'captivating' – as though they have been kidnapped, and spun away to a spacecraft for an indeterminate length of time. One friend wrote to me that it was 'a bathyspheric experience': 'You're let down into this world in which the atmospheric pressures of history build and build, and as you descend, the colouring of the world goes askew, and flattens into greyness. You're safe within the diving-bell yourself, but characters float by who aren't protected, and who are being crushed by the weight of it all.'

The following passage is taken from *The Rings of Saturn*, where the Sebald-not-Sebald narrator (we might call him the 'impersonal author's deputy or delegate', as Henry James decorously described his narrators)[14] is standing on the coast near Southwold, overlooking 'the German Ocean', also known as the North Sea:

> I gazed farther and farther out to sea, to where the darkness was thickest and where there extended a cloudbank of the most curious shape, which I could barely make out any longer, the rearward view, I presume, of the storm that had broken over Southwold in the late afternoon. For a while, the topmost summit regions of this massif, dark as ink, glistened like the icefields of the Caucasus, and as I watched the glare fade I remembered that years before, in a dream, I had once walked the entire length of a mountain range just as remote and just as unfamiliar. It must have been a distance of a thousand miles or more, through ravines, gorges and valleys, across ridges, slopes and drifts, along the edges of great forests, over wastes of rock, shale and snow. And I recalled that in my dream, once I had reached the end of my journey, I looked back, and that it was six o'clock in the evening. The jagged peaks of the mountains I had left behind rose in almost fearful silhouette against a turquoise sky in which two or three pink clouds drifted. It was a scene that felt familiar in an inexplicable way, and for weeks it was on my mind until at length I realized that, down to the last detail, it matched the Vallüla massif, which I had seen from the bus, through eyes drooping with tiredness, a day or so before I started school, as we returned home from an outing to the Montafon.[15]

Notice, first of all, how thought moves here. The shape and glisten of the cloudbank over 'the German Ocean' recalls a real mountain range (the Caucasus), which in turn recalls a mountain range walked in a dream, which in turn recalls a real massif (the Vallüla). There is the hint of a dark submerged mass of childhood memory, which we are not allowed fully to glimpse. It's a trick which Sebald works again and again. Instead of following causal connections between time zones, and between remembrances, his narrator's memory moves by way of visual or formal rhymes: the shapes of the cloudbanks and the mountains echo each other, and this provides the points of contact that are needed for memory to leap across centuries or countries. So often this happens in Sebald: a sudden uncanny sliding occurs, as different pasts slip briefly into alignment. Such elective affinities (Goethe) or family resemblances (Wittgenstein) became, for Sebald, a means of perceiving the past. As he wrote in Austerlitz: 'It does not seem to me that we understand the laws governing the return of the past, but I feel more and more as if time did not exist at all, only various spaces interlocking according to the rules of a higher form of stereometry, between which the living and the dead can move back and forth as they like.' [16] Photographs, for Sebald, also provided these corridors in time, these points of intersection where 'spaces interlocked'. When looking at photographs, he wrote in *The Emigrants*, we feel 'as if the dead were coming back, or as if we were on the point of joining them'.[17]

    The Southwold passage also catches something of the exceptional but ashen beauty with which Sebald was capable of writing. He was attuned, like no other contemporary writer, to the poignancy of transience, and many of his most memorable images concern ebb and recession. But he was also receptive to the peculiar beauties of calamity. In *On The Natural History of Destruction*, for instance, he lavished a contrary, slow, ecstatic description of the firebombing of Hamburg in July 1943, evoking its panorama of deliquescence.[18] In *The Rings of Saturn* he describes, in precise ecstasy, the great British storm of October 1987, when there was 'none of the crashing sounds that go with the felling of timber', and the narrator realizes that:

the trees, held to the last by their root systems, toppled only gradually, and because they were forced down so slowly, their crowns, which were entangled with each other, did not shatter, but remained virtually undamaged. In this way, entire tracts of woodland were pressed flat as if they were cornfields.[19]

Here is another brilliant passage, this time from *Austerlitz*. The title character has returned to Paris to seek evidence of the time his father spent in that city:

Soon I was merely wandering without any aim of plan in mind down the streets leading away from the Boulevard Auguste Blanqui, up to the Place d'Italie on one side and back down to the Glaciere on the other, always thinking, against all reason, that I might suddenly see my father appear out of nowhere, coming towards me or stepping out of an entrance. I sat in this bar too for hours on end, trying to imagine him in his plum-coloured double-breasted suit, perhaps a little threadbare now, bent over one of the café tables and writing those letters to his loved ones in Prague which never arrived... I felt,... said Austerlitz, as if my father were still in Paris and just waiting, so to speak, for a good opportunity to reveal himself. Such ideas infallibly come to me in places which have more of the past about them than the present. For instance, if I am walking through the city and look into one of those quiet courtyards where nothing has changed for decades, I feel, almost physically, the current of time slowing down in the gravitational field of oblivion.[20]

Sebald's sentences are gymnastic, or Escherian. They stand upon each other's shoulders, but also fold back on themselves to become descriptions of each other. They are ramshackle, gothicky, Gormenghasty constructions, haphazardly built – like cloud formations. His sentences, like his characters and like his books, seem to wander without any aim of plan in mind. They disappear down side streets, peer into doorways and buildings. They collect things: stories, images, objects, thoughts, clauses. They are the sentences he wrote of in *The Rings of Saturn*, which 'extend over one or two pages, sentences that resemble processions or a funeral cortège in their sheer ceremonial lavishness'.[21]

Yet for all their grammatical passivity, their crepitations of age, their gentle disregard for active verbs, their slow unfurlings, Sebald's phrases are also unmistakably, to borrow Marianne Moore's statement, 'diction that is... galvanized against inertia'.[22] Among the many quiet paradoxes that attend his work is that his recursive period diction is in fact a dramatically flexible alloy. Despite its apparent age, it is resolutely modern in its ability to speak to us, and to haunt us. It comes, as one critic put it, 'staring [back] at us from an unsuspected vantage point that is decades ahead of the Victorians, and – it takes a chilling moment to realize – ahead of us as well'.[23]

What you also come to understand is that the allergy of Sebald's sentences to anything resembling purpose is itself a form of intent. Long sections of his books – in *The Rings of Saturn* in particular – can leave the reader close to boredom. Where is this going? Why another, apparently disconnected anecdote? And yet if you keep reading, you find that long after you would normally have shut the book you realise that a very different form of momentum is being worked at here; that these are not the bold, pre-ordained trajectories of a conventional novel, but something that is both contingent and deliberate at once.

❉

The best phrase Sebald could come up with to describe the genre he had invented was 'prose fiction', which falls almost laughably short of what he achieved within it. But he was reluctant to call his books 'novels', for he did not want them in any way associated with the crassness of much contemporary fiction.

What did Sebald loathe about contemporary fiction?

He loathed the vulgarly eager way it solicited sympathy for its characters.

He loathed its factual promiscuity, the way it crammed its pages full of unsorted information, googled out of the swill of popular culture, the way it gorged itself on the lipids of data, its excessively high fact content. 'Especially these days, when there is so much information about everything, you have to disregard most of it,' he said. 'You must find a way of ignoring everything else and just follow your nose.'

He found contemptibly comic what he called the 'grinding' noises that 'conventionally plotted' novels required, as they clunkily changed gear, shifted location, or even just moved a character from here to there. He scorned the filler phrases which they used to denote place and action: 'As he sat down at the table, frowning...', 'He called over his shoulder, despairingly....' 'There is', Sebald said, 'so often about the standard novel something terribly contrived, which somewhere along the line tends to falter... The business of having to have bits of dialogue to move the plot along, that's fine for an eighteenth- or nineteenth-century novel, but that becomes in our day a bit trying, where you always see the wheels of the novel grinding and going on.'[24]

What did Sebald do to reform the conventions of contemporary fiction?

In place of character, he substituted climate. His novels have their own weather-systems. They do not enjoy temperatures in the nineties all year round. In *Austerlitz* there is 'miasma',[25] 'impenetrable fog',[26] and the air is 'hatched with grey'.[27] 'Drizzle' pinstripes the pages. In *The Emigrants* there is 'a veil of rain',[28] in *Vertigo* 'veils of ash'.[29] 'All forms and colours', writes Sebald in *Austerlitz*, 'were dissolved in a pearl-grey haze; there were no contrasts, no shading any more, only flowing transitions with the light throbbing through them, a single blur from which only the most fleeting of visions emerged'.[30] Other writers have tried to do the same – think of the Arctic noir of *Miss Smilla's Feeling For Snow*,[31] the leonine summer of Ian McEwan's *Atonement*,[32] the Mittel-Europan tropicality of Wolfgang Koeppen's *The Hothouse*[33] – but none has been as successful as Sebald.

In place of description he substituted black-and-white photographs. Those photographs. Sometimes they take up an entire page, or two pages. They always appear without captions, and this muteness perversely makes them more radiant with meaning. Sebald came upon his images with the same haphazardness with which he found other items of information. They were old postcards, truffle-hunted in book-and-print fairs, or they were clippings from faded newspapers, or they were facsimiled from library collections. Many of them were taken by Sebald himself; he often carried a camera with him.

In place of plot he substituted pattern. Images recur in his work: ramshackle buildings, butterflies or moths, silkworms, mountains, storms, skulls, dust motes. These patterns are like the corrugations on the road before a roundabout; they are there to make us slow down and wake up. Meaning collects in the dips and runnels which these patterns make in the narrative. The patterns are also analogues or enactments of Sebald's large theme – the return of history. 'And so they are ever returning to us, the dead,' he wrote towards the end of the first story in *The Emigrants*.[34]

❊

What is the case against Sebald's work?

That he is the Eeyore of contemporary literature, whose glum pessimism is relentlessly mistaken for profundity. This from A. A. Milne's *The Pooh Book of Quotations:*

> The old grey donkey, Eeyore, stood by himself in a thistly corner of the Forest, his front feet well apart, his head on one side, and thought about things. Sometimes he thought sadly to himself, 'Why?' and sometimes he thought, 'Wherefore?' and sometimes he thought, 'Inasmuch as which?' and sometimes he didn't quite know what he was thinking about.[35]

The case against Sebald can be broken down as follows:

That he has been widely praised for his anti-sentimentalism in writing about the Holocaust and the Second World War, but that his extreme melancholy in fact congeals into a form of sentimentalism.

That the out-of-timeness of his register is little more than a sham or touch-up job. He uses one-coat, quick-dry antiquarianism to make his world seem more distressed than it is. He is a talented retro-fitter, who meticulously mocks up his sentences, oxidises his adjectives, stone-washes his sub-clauses.

That his phrasings have about them the call-centre character of bad German prose, which, by moving the verb towards the end of the sentence, always keeps the reader hanging on for a result which is not worth the wait.

That his characters, including his narrators, are a dynasty of Miss Havishams, living out a gossamery, granular existence, cherishing decay, falling joylessly to bits.

That his carefully meshed patternings are like the filters on a tumble-dryer, they are dense with nothing more significant than historical lint.

That he has been so enthusiastically taken up in Britain and in America because those countries are usually resistant to reading European literature, and that what readers in those countries mistake for a new type of writing is in fact nothing more than an Englished version of common late-nineteenth and early twentieth-century middle-European prose.

That because Sebald deals with themes which seem to be possessed of great moral density – the ethics of memory, the Holocaust, the Second World War – and which are made if not comprehensible at least accessible, and because he does so in a way which is resistant to analysis, we feel that we are being disproportionately enriched by reading him.

That he is a vendor of vagueness, who gestures beautifully to a depth and a grievousness of history which he is unable to describe. He makes his cultural capital out of precisely the sense of history's sublimity which overpowers his characters. Take this from *Austerlitz*: 'I kept thinking, like a madman, that there were mysterious signs and portents all around me here; how it even seemed to me as if the silent facades of the buildings knew something ominous about me.'[36] Or this, from later in the same book: 'Such ideas infallibly come to me in places which have more of the past about them than the present.'[37]

That his photographs are there for cheap special effects. See, for supporting evidence, Sebald's own cultivatedly vague theories on the relationship between his text and his images. In *Austerlitz*: '[there is] the mysterious quality peculiar to such photographs when they surface from oblivion. One has the impression, she said, of something stirring in them, as if one caught small sighs of despair [...] as if the pictures had a memory of their own and remembered us, remembered the roles that we, the survivors, and those no longer among us had played in our former lives'.[38] In a lecture: 'These old photographs always seem to have this appeal written into them, that you should tell a story behind them. In *The Emigrants* there is a group photograph of a large Jewish family, all wearing Bavarian costume. That one image tells you more about the history of German-Jewish aspiration than a whole monograph would do.'[39] In interview: 'Certain things emerge from the images if you look at them long enough.'[40] Well, yes.

Sebald was, like his characters, a collector. Walter Benjamin, himself a hoarder of quotations and of books, remarked that all collections are structured by a 'peculiar category of completeness': the collector tries to overcome the irrational disorder of the world by gathering objects in 'a new, expressly devised historical system: the collection.'[41] Thus it is that the collector's attitude is in 'the highest sense', wrote Benjamin, 'the attitude of an heir'.[42] The collector establishes himself in the past, so as to achieve, undisturbed by the present, 'to renew the old world.'[43] This is the impulse which is shared by Sebald's characters. Faced with a past too overwhelming to contemplate in its whole, his characters desperately select and recombine images and events from their histories to give a finite rhythm and structure to experience. In order to stay sane, they have to pattern images of their origins which simplify and distort them. Their collections act like the pins on a pachinko board. They control, though not always predictably, the way the past drops down to them.

The most oppressed and obsessive of Sebald's characters is his last, Jacques Austerlitz. He is wrecked on the reef of the past. As we learn in the course of the book, he was evacuated to Britain by train on the Kindertransport at the age of four. He was placed in the home of a Welsh Calvinist couple. They raise Austerlitz (and Sebald's evocation of the silent austerity of their house is magnificent) and he succeeds in forgetting his early years. This forgetting, however, comes at the cost of a later breakdown: 'I had,' Austerlitz recalls, 'neither memory nor the power of thought, nor even any existence... all my life had been a constant process of obliteration, a turning away from myself and the world.'[44] In his fifties, Austerlitz begins to recover his memories of having arrived in Britain from Prague on a Kindertransport. This return of the repressed begins with a single image: Austerlitz sees himself as a small boy sitting on a bench in a railroad station.[45] Other memories bud out of this one, and he is moved to return to Europe to search for evidence of the fate of his family. His tour takes him to Terezín (also known as Theresienstadt), an SS-run ghetto in the former Czechoslovakia. While he is wandering around the empty streets of the ghetto, he discovers in a museum that in December 1942, some sixty thousand people were shut up together in the ghetto, a built-up area of one square kilometre at the most, and a little later, when I was out in the deserted town square again, it suddenly seemed to me, with the greatest clarity, that they had never been taken away after all, but were still living crammed into those buildings and basements and attics, as if they were incessantly going up and down the stairs, looking out of the windows, moving in vast numbers through the streets and alleys, and even, a silent assembly, filling the entire space occupied by the air, hatched with grey as it was by the fine rain.[46]

Austerlitz is so distressed by this knowledge that he can barely climb onto the bus which will take him back to Prague. Sebald's works are full of moments like this, when characters are physically disabled by the past, when memory attains an assaulting force.

'To my mind,' Sebald once said, 'it seems clear that those who have no memory have the much greater chance to lead happy lives.' [47] Austerlitz is the archetype of Sebald's people, a model citizen in his principality of greyness, since his identity depends upon his ability to gather fragments of the past to himself. At first it seems that the tragedy of the book – and it is a tragedy which is deeply felt by the reader – is that no matter how thoroughly and long he pursues the reconstruction of his family's life, they will remain wiped out, and he will remain ghostly. By the end of the book, however, we have realised the more awful, more complex, self-involuted nature of Austerlitz's melancholy (and it is the melancholy of all Sebald's characters): that he is driven to preserve his memory in its fragmentariness, for to see the past wholly would be to be destroyed by it.

---

[1] 'The Last Word', Sebald in Conversation with Maya Jaggi, *The Guardian* (21st December, 2001).
[2] 'The Last Word'.
[3] 'The Last Word'.
4 John Banville 'The Rubble Artist' *The New Republic* (26 November 2001), p.38.
5 Walter Benjamin 'The Images of Proust' *Illuminations* (London, Pimlico: 1999), pp.197-210; p.197.

6 James Wood 'The Right Thread' *The New Republic* (6 July 1998), p.38.
7 John Banville et al. 'Books of the Year' *The Irish Times* (1 December 2001), n.p.
8 A. S. Byatt 'Only Connect' *New Statesman* Vol.130, Issue 4559 (15 October 2001), p.52.
9 Lynne Sharon Schwartz et al. 'A Symposium on W.G. Sebald' *The Three Penny Review* Issue 89, (Spring 2002) [online] http://www.threepennyreview.com/samples/sebaldsympos_sp02.html, accessed 28 July 2013.
10 Ozick, Cynthia, 'The Posthumous Sublime' *The New Republic* (16 December 1996), pp.33-8.
11 Tom Paulin in conversation with Amit Chaudhuri *Clearing a Space: Reflections On India, Literature, and Culture* (Oxford, Peter Lang: 2008), p.147.
12 Adam Thirlwell, 'Kitsch and WG Sebald' *Arete* special retrospective issue, No. 40 (Spring/Summer, 2013).
13 Sebald in conversation with Joseph Cuomo in 'A Conversation with W.G. Sebald' *The Emergence of Memory: Conversations with W.G. Sebald*. Ed. Lynne Sharon Swartz (New York, Seven Stories: 2007), pp.93-118; p.94.
14 Henry James 'Preface' *The Golden Bowl* (London. Penguin: 1985), pp.19-38; p.19. First published 1904.
15 *The Rings of Saturn*, p.79.
16 *Austerlitz*, p.261.
17 *The Emigrants*, p.46.
18 *On the Natural History of Destruction*, pp.26-30.
19 *The Rings of Saturn*, pp.266-7.
20 *Austerlitz*, pp.358-9.
21 *The Rings of Saturn*, p.19.
22 Marianne Moore *Predilections* (New York, Viking,:1955), p.4.
23 André Aciman 'Out of Novemberland' *The New York Review of Books* (3 December 1998), n.p.
24 Arthur Lubow citing Sebald during 'A Symposium on W.G. Sebald'.
25 *Austerlitz*, p.248.
26 *Austerlitz*, p.175.
27 *Austerlitz*, p.281.
28 *The Emigrants*, p.128.
29 *Vertigo*, p.51.
30 *Austerlitz*, p.135.
31 Peter Høeg *Miss Smilla's Feeling for Snow* (London, Harvill:1993). First published in Danish 1992.
32 Ian McEwan *Atonement* (London, Jonathan Cape: 2001).
33 Wolfgang Koeppen *The Hothouse* (New York, W.W. Norton: 2001). First published in German 1953.
34 *The Emigrants*, p.23.
35 A.A. Milne *The Pooh Book of Quotations* (London, Methuen Children's Books:1986), p.33.
36 *Austerlitz*, p.304.
37 *Austerlitz*, p.359.
38 *Austerlitz*, p. 258.
39 'The Last Word' n.p.
40 Arthur Lubow citing Sebald during 'A Symposium on W.G. Sebald'.
41 Walter Benjamin *The Arcades Project* (MA, Harvard UP: 1999), pp.204-5.
42 Walter Benjamin 'Unpacking My Library' *Illuminations* (London, Pimlico: 1999), pp.61-9; p.68.
43 'Unpacking My Library', p.63.
44 *Austerlitz*, p.174.
45 *Austerlitz*, pp.200-1.
46 *Austerlitz*, p.281.
47 'The Last Word', n.p.

Gillian Beer

*

Sebald in the City

In the opening pages of *The Rings of Saturn*, Sebald's apparently most bucolic work, we find ourselves standing with him at twilight high up on the eighth floor in the hospital looking way down onto the city of Norwich – a city reduced to silence, with pin figures and toy cars creeping through the hushed landscape. The collision and the distance between observer and place comes as a shock. Instead of the oppressiveness of crowds, the claustrophobia of streets, we encounter the blanked-out stare: 'the familiar city, extending from the hospital courtyards to the far horizon', is 'an utterly alien place'. He is inside that modern cathedral, the hospital, a building that wards and looms above the community it serves. He looks down, as from a cliff, 'upon a sea of stone or a field of rubble, from which the tenebrous masses of multi-story car parks rose up like immense boulders'.[1] As so often in his descriptions, natural history and manmade relics interchange: car-parks need boulders if their shadowy bulk is to be described. The pre-history of the city (the sea of stone) and its making and unmaking (the field of rubble) co-exist in time and space. This is a silent place, not even the wail of the siren prevailing – silent, save for the sound of the wind and the murmur in the narrator's own ears. And although this scene is our first encounter with him, the narrator has arrived in this place a year after the apparently carefree time (which will form the mass of the narrative) 'walking for hours in the day through the thinly populated countryside, which stretches inland from the coast'.[2]

Height is obliterative. Distance erases differences. *The Rings of Saturn*, a work that will ruminate intensely on the oddity of people, the intricacies of past connection, the specificities of individual lives, opens with a panoramic sweep that exterminates the human, enacted in a place of purported salvation, the hospital. Yet salvation of a kind is granted – for in the next paragraph it is yet another year later. The scene in the hospital acts as a time-hinge, or fulcrum, that poises (and unsteadies) recollection. It is a moment very probably forgotten by the reader as we follow the writer's pathways through the countryside. The forgotten silenced city expresses a central paradox in Sebald's work. Cities carry the past and they obliterate it. They are full of people and they void their presences.

Cities mean very differently for incomer and inhabitant. For the inhabitant the city is largely local, focussed in nearby streets and in the invisible presences of buildings and people who once were in those streets: 'where the baker used to be', 'where they pulled down that house to put up the apartment block', 'where Mrs. Brown used to live'. Cities here are communicative: present and past coexist in a conversation that composes layers and striations of reference. And the largesse of familiarity means that the whole web of the city is implicit in the local. For the incomer, on the other hand, cities are received as a series of impressions disjunct, with occasional pinpoint places intensely realised, jostling each other in no particular order. Then there is the returning denizen of the city, neither inhabitant nor stranger, who receives the shock of renewal: known places are intensified by unfamiliarity; fresh patterns, fresh details are seized on by an eye no longer jaded by the everyday.

But what of the city dweller who began in the countryside? - and in another country? For such city dwellers, such sojourners, the city as a living place is always a late-comer to memory, and migration is also the story of childhood left behind. That is the case even for those who move not many miles, as well as those who move across nations or, yet further, across languages. Childhood is the place we have come from and that we cannot get back to; that is what gives the poignancy to those local conversations about the vanished baker's shop.

Sebald's work is full of cities, especially their railway stations and fortifications, yet the temper of his work is not concerned with crowds but solitude – or when crowds, then solitude even magnified. Sebald's narrator is a walker, often alone, or alone in the company of a blurred acquaintance, pacing through the city and sometimes out into suburbs, rarely with a set aim, rather, an urban rambler. Max Ferber in *The Emigrants* relishes his Manchester ventures further and 'further out of the city':

> I passed a long-disused gasworks, a coal depot, a bonemill, and what seemed the unending cast-iron palisade fence of the Ordsall slaughterhouse, a Gothic castle in liver-coloured brick, with parapets, battlements, and numerous turrets and gateways, the sight of which absurdly brought to my mind the name of Haeberlein & Metzger, the Nüremberg Lebkuchen makers; whereupon that name promptly stuck in my head, a bad joke of sorts, and continued to knock about there for the rest of the day.[3]

Two cities are set alongside, Manchester and Nuremberg, and share the curious comfort of naming as a knockabout kind of comedy, 'a bad joke of sorts' without explanation. The slaughterhouse at Ordsall, with its liver-coloured brick and suggestion of 'ordure', and the Christmas cookie 'Lebkuchen' resolve 'absurdly' into a doubled name, 'Haeberlein und Metzger'.

Austerlitz opens with the narrator's first approach 'on a glorious early summer's day to the city of Antwerp, known to me previously only by name'.[4] Names have another form of reality. Soon after he leaves the train he begins to feel unwell and after wandering the streets, their names noted with an uneasy pleasure, he goes to the zoo next to the Centraal Station, first sitting beside the aviary, and then entering the Nocturama in which night animals lead 'their sombrous life behind the glass by the light of a pale moon'.[5] Again names cluster into lists whose charm is their suggestion of an order that cannot quite be identified, suggesting themes rather than taxonomies: the streets are 'Jeruzalemstraat, Nachtegaalstraat, Pelikaanstraat, Paradijsstraat, Immerseelstraat'; the creatures (half-forgotten, re-invented) are 'probably bats and jerboas from Egypt and the Gobi Desert, native European hedgehogs and owls, Australian opposums, pine martens, dormice and lemurs'. Only the racoon lingers in his memory and the staring eyes of several of the creatures – eyes like those also of 'certain painters and philosophers'.[6]

Sentences later the Nocturama merges into the 'Salle des pas perdus', described first by what is not there; no cages for lions or leopards, no 'aquaria for sharks, octopuses and crocodiles'.[7] The droll evenness of tone from the narrator makes this imagined absence seem humdrum, refusing to let us dwell on the oddity of imagining such animal presences in a waiting room for travellers. The matter-of-fact tone suggests that there might be a shared past in which such presences were taken for granted. The few travellers, sitting far apart from each other, come late in the description, after the mirrors and rooftops, and are half-naturalised as dwarf species from the Nocturama:

> the last members of a diminutive race which had perished or been expelled from its home-land, and that because they alone survived they wore the same sorrowful expression as the creatures in the zoo.[8]

Animals and people are alike tinged with mournful fairy-tale, hard to distinguish from each other.

Emerging from this silent crowd is Austerlitz, architectural historian, distinguished from the surrounding passivity by his active observations, responding with pen and paper, in words and sketches, to the magnificent architecture of the room. So the first encounter between Austerlitz, narrator, and reader, moves into a survey of architectural history – the discipline that excavates unrealised plans and lost communalities as much as it does material cities.

The account is punctuated by a strange footnote that declares a kind of guilty dream-laden responsibility for events that happened without the narrator's knowledge and at some distance from his life: the fire that destroyed Lucerne Station during his brief stay there in 1971.[9] This footnote presages the long remainder of the book: it suggests that we can never measure the degree of our responsibilities. The note accepts the magical reasoning that implicates us in events of which we had no knowledge until after they occurred. The deep allusion to being born in Germany in 1944 and bearing the aftermath of all that had occurred there is a sonority that sounds throughout Sebald's work and that clusters particularly on his images of cities.

In *On the Natural History of Destruction* Sebald repeats and quotes himself, framing his earlier perception of the word 'city' in quotation marks that enforce, rather than shift or undermine, his childhood associations:

> In one of my narratives I have described how in 1952 [when he was eight], when I moved with my parents and siblings from my birthplace of Wertach to Sonthofen, nineteen kilometres away, nothing seemed as fascinating as the presence of waste land here and there among the rows of houses, for ever since I had been to Munich, as I said in that passage, few things were so clearly linked in my mind with the word 'city' as mounds of rubble, cracked walls, and empty windows through which you saw the empty air.[10]

The repetition of his earlier passage enforces it. From his earliest experiences onwards, cities are linked to destruction. They figure destruction's terrible beauty. And destruction also sets free the future. Commenting on Hans Erich Nossack's description of the destruction of Hamburg, 'Der Untergang', Sebald expresses sympathy with 'the curious sense of exaltation that sometimes seems to overwhelm Nossack at the sight of the devastation in his native city'.[11] Fascination and pleasure lie close side by side in these descriptions and are hard to disentangle. But Sebald is strikingly free of guilt about this connection, though shadowed by guilt in so many other ways. He is not a native of any city. He retains the incomer's eye. In the passage above, the child's sharp eye for the freedoms of annihilation, 'empty windows through which you saw the empty air', gives a lift to the sentence's end.

That lift towards freedom in the gloom is a repeated gesture in Sebald's writing and one that verges from time to time on merriment. In this way he alerts us to the satisfactions we gain from studying destruction and dissolution and obliges us at least to toy with awkward questions about our relation to this material. He is cautious, for example, about the genre of Trümmer-literatur (the literature of the ruins).[12] He resists the 'temptation to integrate that is perpetuated in traditional literary forms'.[13] The city resists integration, accepts collapse and ruin. But, despite its allure, Sebald is determined to resist ruin too.

The material is for him also always materiel, the willed and dangerous matter of destruction, leading to explosion, disruption, fire, and falling. And the relation between the material and the figured is not sharply distinguished. In *Vertigo* the small boy watches the gallimaufry of old action films and the Pathé news shown each fortnight in the village. The news occurs among 'cavalry irregulars', 'Indians' who 'rode across the limitless plains' and a 'crippled violinist' who 'reeled off a cadenza at the base of a prison wall while his companions filed through the iron bars of his cell window':

> Almost every week we saw the mountains of rubble in places like Berlin or Hamburg, which for a long time I did not associate with the destruction wrought in the closing years of the war, knowing nothing of it, but considered them a natural condition of all larger cities.[14]

Rubble is the 'natural condition' of cities – and of car parks at the opening of *The Rings of Saturn*.

Equally, as he recounts in a late essay, he first knew German cities through a card game they played at home when he was five, called 'Cities Quartet': 'Have you got Oldenburg, we asked, have you got Wuppertal, have you got Worms? I learned to read from these names....' Cities are, first of all, names without content; then, pictures without people:

> In fact in the Cities Quartet, as I reconstruct it from memory, Germany was still undivided – at the time of course I thought nothing of that – and not only undivided but intact, for the uniformly dark brown pictures of the cities, which gave me at an early age the idea of a dark fatherland, showed the cities of Germany without exception as they had been before the war: the intricate gables below the citadel of the Nurnberger Burg, the half-timbered houses of Brunswick, the Holsten Gate of the Old Town in Lubeck, the Zwinger and the Bruhl Terraces.[15]

So for the child, images of the past, darkened but undamaged, and of the rubble-filled present, lie equally alongside each other. He understood the rubble of the cities as ur-alt, a fixed – and recurrent – natural condition. Throughout his childhood and youth he could not imagine travelling to these cities in actuality:

There was no call for excursions to Stuttgart [the nearest city to his village] or any of the other cities that still looked so badly damaged, and so until I left my native land at the age of twenty-one it was still largely unknown territory to me, remote and with something not quite right about it. [16]

Cities, it seems, are reserved for adulthood, and for that endless travelling that is the condition of Sebald's writing.

This essay, 'An Attempt at Restitution', was written for the opening of a House of Literature in Stuttgart in 2001 and the essay concludes by asserting that although there are many kinds of writing 'only in literature, however, can there be an attempt at restitution over and above the mere recital of facts and over and above scholarship'. Restitution here bows to the 'memory of those to whom the greatest injustice was done'. [17] But restitution is for Sebald also always the attempt – thwarted and relished – to stabilise in language what has been lost, what preceded the ruins, what naturalised the ruins. Restitution strives to re-make the material world by which the literary text was surrounded at its initiation. Rather than evoke those now immaterial worlds through crystalline images he works, like Conrad, in the gloom, rummaging through memories that sometimes spring forward, sometimes drift away as they are approached. Yet they cannot die. The figure of the hunter Gracchus, like the flying Dutchman and the wandering Jew, is a figure at once doomed and resilient, seeking death but inveterately living.

Cities, too, inveterately live. Despite changes, in buildings, names, street-scapes, people, the pathways scored by the past continue, and are peopled anew. That inveterate life has supported survival in much imaginative writing. Defoe's Moll Flanders, for example, makes her escape after a robbery, through alleyways and the maze of small streets to places which she shares with the reader, some of which were even then no longer extant and that yet act as the signposts of communal life:

I walked away, and turned into Charterhouse Lane, made off through Charterhouse Yard, into Long Lane, then into Bartholomew Close, so into Little Britain, and through the Newgate Hospital, to Newgate Street.

She tries the trick again:

> In Whitechapel, just by the corner of Petticoat Lane, where the coaches stand that go out to Stratford and Bow, and that side of the country; and another time at the flying Horse without Bishopsgate, where the Cheston coaches then lay. [18]

'Then lay': the appeal is to authenticating communal memory.

Or Thomas Hardy, who trained as an architect and who was involved in much church restoration – which for the Victorians often involved cancelling, extirpating the building's history – could figure communality by what was no longer there for the present eye, as well as what survived against the odds in death.

> Casterbridge [the Wessex market town] announced old Rome in every street, alley, and precinct. It looked Roman, bespoke the art of Rome, concealed dead men of Rome. It was impossible to dig more than a foot or two deep about the town fields and gardens without coming upon some tall soldier or other of the Empire, who had lain there in his silent unobtrusive rest for a space of fifteen hundred years. He was mostly found lying on his side, in an oval scoop in the chalk, like a chicken in its shell; his knees drawn up to his chest; sometimes with the remains of his spear against his arm; a fibula or brooch of bronze on his breast or forehead; an urn at his knees, a jar at his throat, a bottle at his mouth; and mystified conjecture pouring down upon him from the eyes of Casterbridge street boys and men, who had turned a moment to gaze at the familiar spectacle as they passed by. [19]

The Roman soldier, past sojourner, has become native inhabitant over time: a 'familiar spectacle' in all his mystery. We can hear in Hardy too the sonorities of Sebald's favourite work, Thomas Browne's *Hydriotaphia, Urn Burial, or a Discourse of the Sepulchral Urns lately found in Norfolk*.[20] The dead survive just beneath our feet, hidden in familiar landscape.

But long history is not, for Sebald, any particular matter for rejoicing. Near the end of *Austerlitz* the narrator is taken up to 'the eighteenth floor of the south-east tower' in the Bibliothéque Nationale:

where one can look down from the so-called belvedere at the entire urban agglomeration which has risen over the millennia from the land beneath its foundations, which is now entirely hollowed out: a pale limestone range, a kind of execrescence extending the concentric spread of its incrustations far beyond the boulevards Davout, Soult, Poniatowski, Massena and Kellermann, and on into the outermost periphery beyond the suburbs, which now lay in the haze of twilight.[21]

As so often in Sebald's work, the litany of names momentarily stays time even as it speaks space and history. (In *Austerlitz*: "Angel Alley, Peter Street, Sweet Apple Court and Swan Yard had all gone").[22]

Like the hospital, the library allows him to look down from a great height on the city. Paris is geometric, unlike medieval Norwich, but from above both have a hint of the cadaver. Here the gaze is succeeded by one of Sebald's vast enwrapped sentences that seem to enact the processes of memory: sometimes maddening, even orotund they may be, but mesmerising. Through them one enters the vertiginous spirals of private recollection re-cast under the pressures of multiple third-person. The single consciousness bears the weight of the communal past and present, of somatic experience shared by all, and it cannot exist without that leakage.

Again, as in the vision of Norwich from the hospital, silence prevails:

> It was strange, said Lemoine, but up here he always had the impression that life moved silently and slowly down below, that the body of the city had been infected by an obscure disease spreading underground, and I remembered, said Austerlitz, when Lemoine made this remark, the winter months of the year 1959 during which I was studying the six-volume work pointing me the way in my own research, on *Paris, ses organs, ses fonctions et sa vie dans la seconde moitié du XIXeme siècle*, which Maxime du Camp, who had previously travelled the deserts of the Orient that are formed, as he said, from the dust of the dead, began to write around 1890, after he was inspired by an overwhelming vision on the Pont Neuf, and which he finished only seven years later.[23]

Organs, functions, and life: the Paracelsian equivalence of human being and universe, here human being and city, shows through at intervals in his writing, particularly in *Austerlitz*.

That long somatic presence of the city is realised as incantation in his writing. In the uttering of lists of streets and alleyways, boulevards and bus stops, all fear of straining and inadequacy is, for a little, laid aside. Indeed, at his lowest point of depression, Austerlitz describes his condition, struggling with language, as being like a man who has been abroad a long time and cannot find his way through this urban sprawl any more, no longer knows what a bus stop is for, or what a back yard is, or a street junction, an avenue or a bridge. The entire structure of language, the syntactical arrangement of parts of speech, punctuation, conjunctions, and finally even the nouns denoting ordinary objects were all enveloped in impenetrable fog.

Language, he suggests:

> may be regarded as an old city full of streets and squares, nooks and crannies, with some quarters dating from far back in time while others have been torn down, cleaned up and rebuilt, and with suburbs reaching further and further into the surrounding countryside. [24]

Perhaps it is that sense of an invisible, vanishing ground plan, as much as the volatile nature of words describing things, that makes for the feeling of risk in reading Sebald. Vertigo haunts and tempts the outer reaches of our consciousness as we make our way, held steady by his serpentine sentences, through the indomitable sequentiality of narrative, leaning against the current of time. Photographs usurp and dissolve the past, sapping signification, yet intensifying the poignancy of what's lost. Light freezes and holds time. Light can also kill. A recurrent image in his work, as frequent in his descriptions of villages as of towns or cities or theatres, is fire: fire that consumes, that flames and rolls onward, that ends in ash. Fire devours life and is life.

Vertigo's last section 'Il ritorno in patria' comes to rest (after his long sojourn at W., his childhood village re-visited among the foothills of the Alps) in London. He pursues an exhausting walk from the National Gallery (where he sees Pisanello's painting of St. George and the Dragon) to 'the western perimeter of the City'. That capitalised (in both senses) City within the city of London is the power-house of finance. He skirts it to reach Liverpool Street station on his way home (we suppose) to unnamed Norwich. He eyes his fellow-travellers with droll dismay:

> There was no room for doubt, however, about the reality of my poor fellow travellers, who had all set off early that morning neatly turned out and spruced up, but were now slumped in their seats like a defeated army and, before turning to their newspapers, were staring out at the desolate forecourts of the metropolis with fixed unseeing eyes. [25]

Sebald turns not to the newspaper but first to dream and then to a book, a book read not now in the present journey but returning to him as memory, 'fragments from the Great Fire of London as recorded by Samuel Pepys':

> We saw the fire grow. It was not bright, it was a gruesome, evil, bloody flame, sweeping before the wind, through all the city. Pigeons lay destroyed upon the pavements, in hundreds, their feathers singed and burned. A crowd of looters roams through Lincoln's Inn. The churches, houses, the woodwork and the building stones, ablaze at once....

Notice the change of tense to the present as the passage, and the fire, expands: 'A crowd of looters roams through Lincoln's Inn'; 'We flee onto the water'. The last sentence is 'And, the day after, a silent rain of ashes, westward, as far as Windsor Park'.[26] Suburbs, City, parkland, royalty, all come under the rain of ash, verbless, and so without end. The book itself ends in passage, in the train, between seventeenth century London and now – a never ceasing passage, because writing unleashes experience which returns, even when the words that began the experience are no longer remembered. This surely is the full meaning for Sebald of restitution and why literature alone can perform it: never enough, always fragmentary, but figuring anew, making anew, in the present of reading, that which has been lost.

The city is always being destroyed, and is always, grudgingly, there still, indefatigable: as Dr. K muses: 'The most disconcerting part of it, perhaps, is that life nevertheless always goes on, somehow or other.'[27] Like the sea, or the human body, to both of which the city is often compared in these books, the city endlessly renews itself, depleted, superb, brick, concrete, rubble, stone and space. And people? Sometimes, in his work, that seems doubtful. Yet the cities that Sebald's narrator visits throng, equally, with those who survive, and the dead. 'They are still around us, the dead, but there are times when I think that perhaps they will soon be gone.' In *Campo Santo* his fear is the fear of losing the dead:

> What must it be like in the cities inexorably moving towards the thirty million mark? Where will they all go, the dead of Buenos Aires and Sao Paolo, of Mexico City, Lagos and Cairo, Tokyo, Shanghai and Bombay? Very few of them, probably, into a cool grave. And who has remembered them, who remembers them at all? [28]

One might respond that each of these cities has its own ritual for sustaining the presence of the dead, whether through the Day of the Dead or the funeral pyre that leads on to re-incarnation. The nostalgia for the cool grave owes much, again, to Thomas Browne. Sebald seems inconsolable: for him, cities are litanies of loss. But the reader, and the writer too, finds comfort in these lists, names rolling off the tongue: 'Have you got Oldenburg we asked; Have you got Wuppertal? Have you got Worms? I learnt to read from these names.' Onomastics provides the haven of retreat into childhood, the time when for him cities were names, and names only.

The dissonance between naming and suffering tugs at Sebald persistently: sometimes that dissonance is tragic, but, equally, it is the source of that rueful merriment that haunts all Sebald's writing. His narrator (and he himself as writer) remains country-dweller and wanderer. He is sometimes close to the hunter Gracchus. But in whatever manifestation he is never at home in the city. So he is able to scan its horizons, refuse its pomp, relish its squalor, but turn again and again to 'empty windows through which you saw the empty air'.

[1] *The Rings of Saturn*, p 5.
[2] *The Rings of Saturn*, p 3.
[3] *The Emigrants*, pp.159-60.
[4] *Austerlitz*, p.1.
[5] *Austerlitz*, p.2.
[6] *Austerlitz*, pp 2-3.
[7] *Austerlitz*, p 5.
[8] *Austerlitz*, p.6.
[9] *Austerlitz*, p 10-11.
[10] *On the Natural History of Destruction*, p.74.
[11] 'Between History and Natural History: On the Literary Description of Total Destruction.' *Campo Santo*, p.77.
[12] 'Between History and Natural History', p.69.
[13] 'Between History and Natural History', p.89.
[14] *Vertigo*, p.187.
[15] 'An Attempt at Restitution.' *Campo Santo* p.207.
[16] 'An Attempt at Restitution', p.209.
[17] 'An Attempt at Restitution', p.214.
[18] Daniel Defoe, *Moll Flanders* (London, J.M. Dent: 1930), p.206. First published January 1722.
[19] Thomas Hardy, *The Mayor of Casterbridge* (London, Macmillan:1974), p.97. First published 1886.
[20] Sir Thomas Browne, *Hydriotaphia, Urn Burial, or a Discourse of the Sepulchral Urns lately found in Norfolk*, ed. Sir Geoffrey Keynes (London, Faber and Faber: 1968) pp 113-157. First published 1658.
[21] *Austerlitz*, p.399.
[22] *Austerlitz*, p.186.
[23] *Austerlitz*, pp.399-400.
[24] *Austerlitz*, pp.174-5.
[25] *Vertigo*, p.260.
[26] *Vertigo*, pp.262-3.
[27] *Vertigo*, p.143.
[28] 'Campo Santo.' *Campo Santo*, pp.34-35.

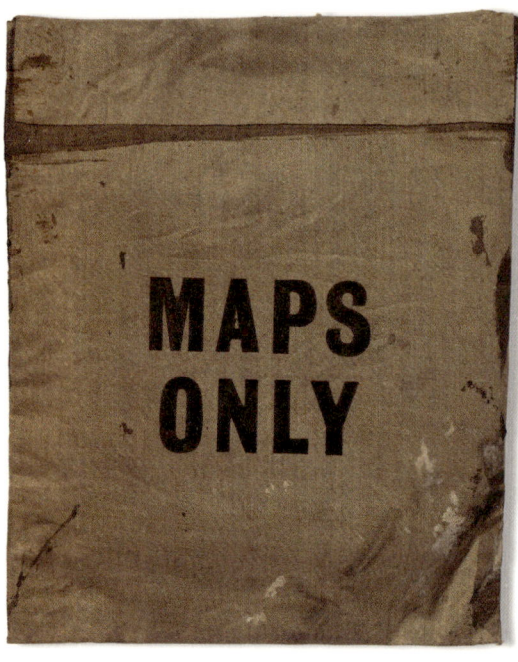

Map found by Joseph Dean in Goch, 1944. Photograph: J. Littkemann

Tacita Dean

*

W.G. Sebald

At Christmas two years ago, I was given a reproduction silk map of the city of Berlin. Seeing the map triggered a memory for my father. He was a Captain in the 51st Highland Division as it moved slowly through Holland into Germany in the Allied advance late in 1944. He remembers seeing a flat expanse of land bordering the river, across which, he recounts, his four guns had just fired a small high explosive barrage as part of an air landing exercise on the other bank. They watched the planes flying over, and when they came back, he saw that one of them was smoking, and to his horror, losing height and heading straight towards him. He couldn't bear to see it crash, so ducked into his slit trench. The plane crashed into muddy soil about a hundred yards away, and when he ran over, the only recognisable object was an envelope lying on the ground marked 'map'.

And then my father went upstairs and returned, remarkably quickly, with the map he had kept for 57 years, which he gave to me. The envelope was made of what felt like rubberised cotton and had the words 'MAPS ONLY' printed on the front. Inside was a large folded silk map of Germany and its border with Holland and France. They were made for pilots from the Royal Air Force, and printed on silk so as not disintegrate in water. We opened up the map, poignantly unused, and my father tried to find the place where he had found it. 'There,' he said pointing to a tiny dot, 'there: I found it in Goch.'

I was in Amsterdam for the palindrome date of 20. 02. 2002. The following morning, I caught an early train to Arnhem, where I was picked up at the station by Rita Kersting, Director of the Kunstverein in Düsseldorf, the gallery where I was going to have a show later in the year. We drove to the Kröller-Müller

Left. Found photographs of Goch, 1944; Right. Goch, 2003 Photographs: Dr. Georg Kersting

Museum in Otterlo. It was a clear February day, and everything felt tamed and safe and comfortable as Holland often does. We went to see the exhibition of Dan Graham, and afterwards drove back through the wooded parkland heading for Düsseldorf.

Somewhere near Nijmegen, we got lost trying to find the autobahn. We drove in the dusk around and around in those lands straddling the border: strange petrol stations, new woods and neat housing. We didn't know which country we were in. Rita told me that she came from a town also quite near to the Dutch border, which was so small I would not have heard of it. I don't know what it was about that landscape and that place, and the atmosphere of that

Photographs of the bombing of Goch, taken from the film, *Krieg am Niederrhein* by Heinz Bosch and Wilhelm Haas, 1981 Courtesy Kreis Kleve © Imperial War Museum OPF 190 (stills not provided by IWM)

strategies. And then I read about Casement's involvement in the struggle for an independent Ireland...

The facts are well known: with the outbreak of the First World War, both the Ulster Volunteer Force and the Irish Volunteers were instructed to join up and fight for Britain against Germany. There was great disillusion amongst the Volunteers who refused to fight for a nation that was, in their opinion, actively oppressing Irish Nationalism. So a breakaway group was formed, and a plan was hatched to ask the Germans for support in their fight for Home Rule and an envoy was dispatched to secure arms. That envoy was Roger Casement.

Sebald writes with great tenderness about Roger Casement: the exhausted man, far too old and unwell to be wading through icy water, who was dropped off by a German submarine on the southwest coast of Ireland after having failed his mission. He had only managed to acquire one tenth of what he had asked for, and had just time to send a message to Dublin to try and call off the uprising, which, in the end, no one heeded. He was too weak to run away, and took refuge

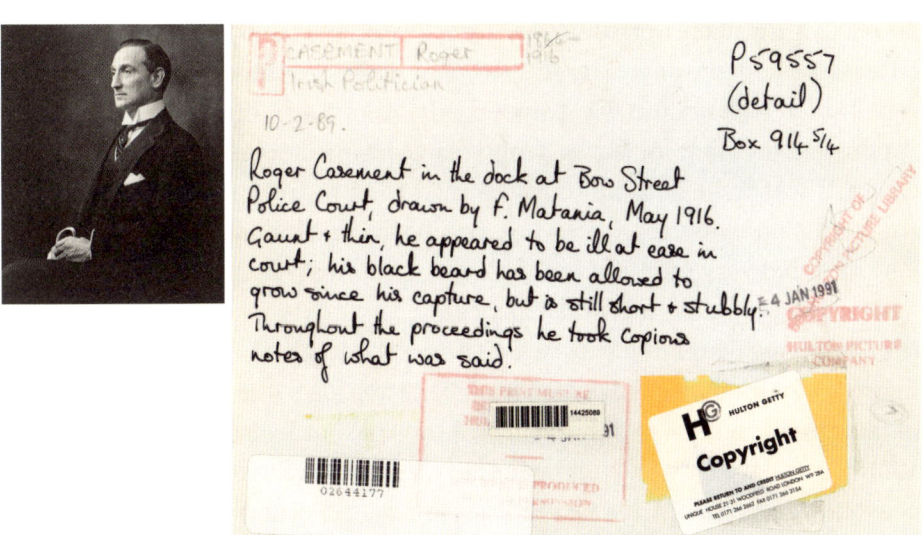

Above. *Rufus Isaacs, 1st Marquess of Reading* Photograph by Walton Adams, 1910 © National Portrait Gallery, London; Right. Reverse side of the Hulton Archive Roger Casement photograph © Getty Images, Hulton Archive

in McKenna's Fort where he was found by a local Constable and arrested. The boat carrying the arms, *Aud Norge*, disguised as a Norwegian merchant ship, waited off the coast of County Kerry for land signals, but none came. Eventually, it was intercepted by the Royal Navy and told to head for Cork. And, as pre-arranged in such a circumstance, the crew put back on their German naval uniforms, raised their flag and surrendered, scuttling the boat as they did so, and detonating the charges off Daunt's Rock.

At his trial at the Old Bailey, Casement acted for his own defence and, according to Sebald, the Counsel for the prosecution was the very man, Frederick Smith, who had led the Ulster Protestants to defeat the Home Rule proposal in 1914. Any pleas for clemency, which came from many quarters in Britain and America because of his distinguished career, were dissipated by the circulation of the so-called Black Diaries, an alternative journal he wrote alongside his public White Diaries that graphically documented a hitherto unimagined homosexuality. Copies were sent to the Archbishop of Canterbury and Arthur Conan Doyle amongst others, and were also used to discredit him in the Congo and quash any likely uprising there were he executed. Now it is known from a letter Casement wrote in March 1916, that he had serious misgivings about a rebellion in Ireland, but was trapped into accepting German conditions for supporting the affair for fear of being seen to have sabotaged the arms deal. He wrote, 'I was to be held up to my countrymen in Ireland and America for something far worse than a coward…my position is hideous.'

From that very moment in the drawing room at Glendun Lodge, when I first heard account of Roger Casement's life, I found it very difficult to reconcile the conflicting truths in his story. Yet I am very attracted to him as an historical figure, and even though I can see the obvious treason to the British government of landing in a German submarine off the coast of Ireland during the First World War, I wish he had not been executed in the climate he was: where no account was given for what he had achieved in Africa, and where all those who supported and respected him were hushed into a conspiratorial homophobia. And so it was that I learnt, as I read Sebald's moving chapter in the bus shelter in Fiji, that the presiding judge who put on the black cap for Roger Casement,

Tacita Dean in the bus stop, Naselesele, Fiji
Photograph: Mathew Hale

moment, which made me ask, quite suddenly, if she came from Goch?

So then we went to Goch, one evening later in the year, to have dinner with Rita's parents, both doctors now retired. Their house had been their practice, so intervening doors were now being permanently sealed up, and those years of service to the community of Goch put away. Rita's father, Georg, was evacuated to Ossendorf on December 6th 1944 when Goch was declared a red zone. He was ten years old. When he returned nine months later in September 1945, his town was ruined. His most enduring memory was of walking in through the normal door of the church and looking up at the ceiling, and there being nothing there but sky. The steeple had been used as a lookout, and was blown up not by the Allies, it seems, but by the retreating Germans fearing its appropriation. He remembers being most shocked by a display of photographs in a shop window taken by British war journalists that were for sale. It was only then that he saw the piles of rubble in the market place, and the unrecognisable state of his hometown.

W. G. Sebald wrote, in an article published in *The New Yorker* after his death in 2001, about the very strange place the bombing of German cities has in the collective memory of the people. He writes not only of the extraordinary efficiency

Right. Katy English in the drawing room of Glendun Lodge
Below. Exterior of Glendun Lodge.
Photographs: Philip English

and speed with which the rubble was cleared and reconstruction begun, but also of the protective amnesia that settled in after the air raids finally ended. As if, he writes, 'the images of this horrifying chapter of our history have never really crossed the threshold of the national consciousness'.[1] Most documented observations, he continues, were made by foreign journalists and writers, repulsed at the damage inflicted by them on a civilian population, whereas in Germany itself, there was near silence.

In September 1999, I was in Fiji recording 24 hours of continuous sound in the bus shelter of the village of Naselesele, Taveuni Island. The sound, wild sound of a particular place with a longitude of 180º, was for a project situated outside the much-unloved Millennium Dome in London. I sat in the bus shelter, with my digital recorder next to me, reading W. G. Sebald's *The Rings of Saturn*. I remember the situation well because I remember what I read. I remember the village in front of me – houses spread out on a grass incline covered with small flowering trees, and the hundreds of children whose excited voices I recorded. It had rained the night before and everything was vivid, and I started to read about Roger Casement.

I had first learnt about Roger Casement from Katy English. I was staying with her in their house in Cushendun, County Antrim – a wonderful old-fashioned place where I often went in the autumn. We were sitting in the drawing room one afternoon, where, Katy told me, Roger Casement would often come to tea with the house's former occupant, Ada McNeill. Ada McNeill lived at Glendun Lodge on grace and favour from her brother Lord Cushendun. She was a woodcarver, and a keen walker who carried a gun wherever she went, shooting up into the sky to scare off boys scrumping for apples. She was also a fervent nationalist, and held quite a candle for Roger Casement, although her sexuality was as undiscussed as his own. She is even rumoured to have buried guns for him in her garden.

Roger Casement's Protestant father and Catholic mother died when he was still quite young, so he was brought up by his aunt and would often stay with his relatives in County Antrim; he also attended the Ballymena Academy. The Casement family land was, and still is, near by Cushendun in the direction of Ballycastle, and his favourite ever place, he wrote to his cousin Gertrude Bannister from Pentonville prison, was the old church ruin of Drumnakill looking over Murlough Bay. Some historians believe it to be the site of the thirteenth station

Postcard from Murlough Bay, Co. Antrim © Ulster Card Company Ltd

Roger Casement in the dock at Bow Street Court, May 1916
Drawing by F. Matania
© Getty Images, Hulton Archive

of the cross on an ancient pilgrim walk, and it is here that a memorial was built to Roger Casement, which has been so badly vandalised that all that remains of it today is a concrete base and a metal prong.

So I read in my bus stop idyll about Casement's meeting with Joseph Conrad, which so impressed the latter that he believed he was the only man of integrity he had met amongst all the Europeans in the Congo. And I read about the report that Casement delivered to the British Foreign Service on the atrocities committed at the hands of the white imperialist enterprise on the black labour force that was such a shocking revelation it forced Belgium to reassess its colonial and uttered those terrifying words that I can hardly bear to write: –'You will be taken hence to a lawful prison and thence to a place of execution and will be there hanged by the neck until you be dead...' was my great, great uncle, Sir Rufus Isaacs.

There were nine children born to the union of Sara Davis and Joseph Isaacs. Rufus was the fourth: Frances, Nelly and Harry were older, and Albert, Florence, Godfrey, Frederick and Esther were younger. Florence was my great, great grandmother.

The family tree, which my uncle produced for me, is a beautiful document on several sheets of folded paper, neatly inscribed in his hand. On the top left side is 'Isaac (? in Germany)', and on the top right is 'Aron Mendoza – Ritual Slaughterer – c. 1725'. Aron was a Sephardic Jew from Portugal, who wrote a book in Hebrew about prize fighting. Both his son and grandson seemed to have carried on the family profession, while his daughter, named Pyra, 'exorcised evil spirits' as her trade. The tree spreads out: still on the right hand side, I trace the lines down to Aron's prize fighting grandson, Daniel, who had eleven children of his own, one of whom, Welcome Mendoza, was grandmother to one Peter Sellers '(actor)'. On the left hand side, I read that Isaac (? in Germany)'s son Michael settled at Chelmsford in England at some point at the beginning of the eighteenth century. The two sides meet eventually some hundred years later, on the fold of the paper, with the marriage of Sara Mendoza to Michael Isaacs '(fruit brother)' who were grandparents to Rufus and his siblings.

From what I can tell, the Isaacs were a close knit family. Joseph Isaacs was a fruit merchant like his father, and his eldest son, Harry, later took over the business. Rufus trained as a lawyer and entered Parliament as a Liberal in 1904, becoming Attorney General in 1910. His brother, Godfrey, became Managing Director of the Marconi Telegraph Company, both in Britain and America. Esther and Florence studied painting together in Paris at the height of Impressionism, and we still have some of Esther's paintings on the walls at home.

In 1912, Rufus and his brother Godfrey were both involved in The Marconi Scandal. The Liberal Government, under Herbert Asquith, had approved of a plan to erect a series of wireless stations around the British Empire, and the

Picture of Godfrey Isaacs from *Mayfair Magazine*, October 9th 1915 © Marconi Corporation plc

contract was put out to tender. A year later, it was agreed to offer the work to the Marconi Telegraph Company. During that winter, articles started to appear in the press, most notably in the political weekly *The Eye Witness* by such writers as Cecil Chesterton and Hilaire Belloc, clearly implying that Rufus Isaacs, Lloyd George and other members of the Cabinet had profited from insider knowledge about the contract.

Both brothers sued for libel and won, Rufus against a French newspaper, which openly accused him and the Postmaster General, H. L. Samuel, of corruption, and Godfrey against Cecil Chesterton. The cases brought the issue to public attention, and in 1913, Rufus Isaacs and Lloyd George were asked to make statements to a Committee explaining their actions. It appeared that Rufus had in fact bought ten thousand Marconi shares from another brother, Harry Isaacs, but they were from the American company, not the British one. He, in turn, sold a portion of them to Lloyd George, Samuels and the Chief Liberal Whip, Lord Murray, who even acquired some for the Liberal

Party. The Ministers stated to the Committee that as the American company would not benefit directly from the contract, they believed it to be an entirely private transaction.

In June 1913, it was decided that charges of gross corruption were unfounded, but that the Ministers had been ill advised in buying the shares and delaying the disclosure of the facts. No blame was imputed to anyone except to those who had circulated the charges of corruption. However, the vote was not unanimous. The Unionist members held that the Ministers had acted with grave impropriety, and forced the issue into a debate in the House of Commons. Rufus Isaacs and Lloyd George, while protesting good faith, admitted their error of judgement, and a motion was passed accepting their statements by 346 votes to 268.

When I asked my father about the affair, he told me that Rufus had always maintained to his sister Florence that the reason he had been less than candid about the shares was that he was advised to be so by Lloyd George. Whatever the story, the scandal did unleash a wave of anti-Semitism, particularly addressed at the Jewish 'ringleaders' of the affair: Rufus, Godfrey and H. L. Samuel. This reached its most insidious point with the publication of a vicious hate poem by Rudyard Kipling called, *Gehazi*, directly addressing Rufus's subsequent promotion to Lord Chief Justice in 1913 comparing him to the rapacious and cunning Biblical character, Gehazi, who was cursed with leprosy for betraying his master. The poem ends:

> What means the risen whiteness,
> Of the skin between thy brows?
> The boils that shine and burrow,
> The sores that slough and bleed-
> The leprosy of Naaman
> On thee and all thy seed?
> Stand up, stand up, Gehazi,
> Draw close thy robe and go,
> Gehazi, Judge in Israel,
> A leper white as snow! [2]

Gugliemo Marconi supported his Managing Director throughout The Marconi Scandal; they seem to have been very close colleagues. When Godfrey died, just months after retiring from the company due to ill health and overwork, Marconi's letter of condolence to his widow is so scored out as to appear grief stricken. When he took over the position in 1910, Godfrey was zealous in his enforcement of the company's patents, which gave him the reputation of being a litigious man, but evidently his energy, business intelligence, and enthusiasm for the new science, coupled with Marconi's inventive brilliance, were fundamental in establishing wireless communication in Britain.

Guglielmo Marconi with Godfrey Isaacs attending the court enquiry into the disaster of the sinking of the *Titanic*, 1912
© Marconi Corporation plc

Marconi was born in Bologna, but his mother was Irish. Inspired by the discovery that electromagnetic waves exist in the air, he began experimenting, and lodged the first patent for 'wireless technology' in 1896. Two years later, Lloyds of London invited him to experiment with overseas wireless links over the small stretch of water between Ballycastle and Rathlin Island in County Antrim. Marconi sent his assistant, George Kemp, who after various trials managed to receive the first radio signal ever transmitted over sea. As it happened, it was across the very bay that Roger Casement found so dear and which is overlooked today by his broken monument. Also, ironically, it is where U-19, the very same German submarine which had brought Casement home two years before, torpedoed and sank the armed merchant cruiser, HMS Calgarian, with the loss of 49 lives.

It was evidently a particular concern of Marconi's to end isolation at sea, and one of his first moves with the advancement of his technology was to put radio operators on board ships. These men were often radio enthusiasts and were employed, not by the shipping companies, but by Marconi himself. It was an expensive business that used a lot of electricity with long aerials strung up the ship's masts. Weather conditions dictated how far a signal could travel, and

National Cabinet Group, August 31st 1931 Photograph by James Jarché © Daily Herald Archive / Science & Society Picture Library

it was often easier to work at night. Initially, the technology seems to have been much more attractive to First Class passengers with money to spend on sending greetings to those at home, than to captains accustomed to silence at sea. Messages would hopscotch from boat to boat until they reached land. It was also fairly common not to signal to boats using rival technology, namely not the Marconi brand. Business competition at sea was rife.

All this is what went wrong, as well as right, on the evening of April 14th 1912 when Titanic hit an iceberg somewhere in the north Atlantic. Radio operator Harold Bride seems to have prioritised sending the passengers' messages over an incoming ice warning from another ship, Californian. There was no direct communication to the bridge, so subsequent ice warnings were not passed on. However, after the collision, he did manage to get a distress warning to three ships including Carpathia, which arrived in time to save 700 lives, but the operator of Californian, the closest ship by over a hundred miles, had already gone to bed.

At the enquiry into the Titanic disaster, presided over by Rufus Isaacs, who was still the Attorney General at that time, Marconi wireless technology was pronounced the saver of many lives. Twenty-four hour wireless watch became mandatory at sea and the price of Marconi shares rapidly appreciated. But such a commentator and seamen as Joseph Conrad could only look cynically upon

Intérieur du Café Carrel, Arles by Vincent Van Gogh, Arles, August 1888 Oil on canvas. Courtesy of James Roundell, London

such a misadventure, as he wrote in 1912 in his observation, *Some Reflections, Seaman-like and otherwise, on the loss of the Titanic*:

> ...to the applause of two continents, you launch that mass with 2,000 people on board at 21 knots across the sea - a perfect exhibition of the modern blind trust in mere material and appliances... if that luckless ship had a couple of feet shorter, she would probably have gone clear of the danger. But then, perhaps, she could not have had a swimming bath and a French café: a sort of marine Ritz, proclaimed unsinkable and sent adrift with its casual population upon the sea, without enough boats, without enough seamen ... [3]

My father and uncle both have memories of Rufus, a kindly but sharply intelligent old man, who was much happier after his second marriage to his secretary, Stella Charnaud. He was made Viceroy of India at the time when Gandhi was gaining prominence in 1921, and then returned to be Foreign Secretary in Ramsay MacDonald's 1931 National coalition government.

His sister Florence married a business acquaintance of her brother Harry's in the fruit trade, who was always called Tommy in the family but born Albert Van Gruisen. His father was a Dutchman, and grandson of the famous Friesland organ builder, Albertus Van Gruisen; his mother was English. They were my great, great grandparents.

Their youngest sister Esther married the playwright Alfred Sutro but they had no children. In 1896, while on a trip to Paris, Esther bought from the Ambroise Vollard Gallery in Rue Lafitte a painting by Vincent Van Gogh. The painting was called, *Interieur du Cafe Carrel, Arles*, which he had painted in 1888, just two years before he died. She became its first owner, and brought the painting back to England where it hung in her home at Chester Terrace. My father remembers the painting as a large oil scene 'with those restaurant chairs he painted so often'. Great-aunt Essie, as she was known to him, died intestate in 1934 and the painting was passed on briefly to her sister Florence Van Gruisen. She sold it in 1935, much to the perpetual regret of the family, for about £2500, and divided the proceeds amongst the remaining Isaacs siblings.

I decided to track it down, and looked through all his paintings for scenes that matched my father's childhood memory. Only when I took to the Internet and typed in 'Goch' instead of 'Gogh' did it occur to me that his family might well have come from the German town at the heart of this narrative. In the introduction to the 1953 edition of *The Collected Letters of Vincent Van Gogh*, his sister-in-law Jo van Gogh-Bonger confirms this by explaining that the family name, 'Van Gogh', derives from the small German town on the Dutch border, and that it is a name which has existed since the sixteenth century.

In my search for the painting, I came up with three options: three restaurant interiors, one painted in Paris and two in Arles. The Parisian scene was in the collection of the Kröller-Müller Museum. Could we have inadvertently looked upon Esther's Van Gogh that afternoon in February? In the end, I discovered through its provenance that it was one of the other two Arles paintings, and that its current whereabouts appeared clouded in a great and mysterious secrecy, which has taken the help of several experts to unravel.

It was sold in 1935 through the Lefevre Gallery to America where it stayed in Providence, Rhode Island until it appeared at a Christie's auction in 1996.

The presentation of the Heine Prize to W.G. Sebald in the Senate Room of County Hall in the City of Düsseldorf by the Mayor Joachim Erwin on December 13th 2000.
Photograph by Wilfried Meyer

It was then sold once more for over ten million dollars to a London dealer, who was formerly the Christie's specialist on Impressionism. Who they sold it to after that, when, and for how much was of the utmost sensitivity, I was told. And only yesterday, on the eve of finishing this text, did I learn that *Interieur du Cafe Carrel, Arles* is back in America and currently somewhere in Texas, apparently promised one day to the Kimbell Art Museum in Fort Worth.

So that February evening, we found our way onto the autobahn, and arrived in Düsseldorf well after dark. I learnt later, the city had invited Sebald to receive the Heinrich Heine award, exactly a year and a day before he was killed in a car accident in Norfolk on 14 December 2001. In photographs, taken that day by the town hall, Sebald looks awkward and wary of such civic formalities, as he uncomfortably holds open, with the help of the mayor, the oversized book displaying the laudation; the flash having bleached out any details written inside it.

Postscript*

Just over three weeks ago, I drove to London from Berlin on my way to Kent. I woke up that first morning to hear on the radio that a painting of the Appeal of Roger Casement was due to go on show to the public the following day in the National Portrait Gallery. It was a news event. I was surprised as one of my starting points in the writing of 'W. G. Sebald' had been to try and locate a drawing of Casement which had once appeared in a newspaper and which I'd had pinned up above my desk for some time. My research had started in the National Portrait Gallery, where it appeared they only had two awkward pencil drawings by Sir William Rothenstein in their collection, drawn in 1911 around the time of Casement's knighthood.

So I went in that afternoon to look at *High Treason, Court of Criminal Appeal: the Trial of Roger Casement 1916* painted by John Lavery. It was a large painting, recently cleaned – the action strangely inert and dull. The painter had been

High Treason, Court of Criminal Appeal: the Trial of Sir Roger Casement 1916
Sir John Lavery, 1916. Oil on canvas. © UK Government Art Collection

sitting in the empty jury box opposite and facing Casement, who sat alone looking back. Everyone else is uncomfortably foreshortened and squashed into the picture plane. They are preoccupied, and in profile, as they focus on the Bench to the left of the painting. Only one other person, I noticed, had her face turned towards the painter. She too is looking out, but her eyes are not defiant like those of Casement, but slightly downcast. I looked at the crude key to identify her, and was taken aback to see that it was Ada McNeill.

It was the presiding Appeal Judge, a Unionist supporter named Darling, who had personally commissioned the painting. A friend of the artist, he had invited Lavery to document his role in an event he believed would be the most important State Trial of the Century. Not a stranger to vanity, he had already had himself depicted once before by Lavery in full judicial robes and black cap, pronouncing a death sentence. That painting was thought by many to be in bad taste, and the Casement one also attracted criticism, which might be the reason why it was never finished at the time, and ended up still in Lavery's possession. It was bequeathed on his death in 1941 to the National Portrait Gallery but was declined, although it was kept there until the end of the War. It was then offered to the Royal Courts of Justice, who accepted it, with some embarrassment, and was eventually hung in 1947 out of public view in a room occupied by the Clerk to the Registrar of Criminal Appeals.

In 1950, Serjeant Sullivan, who had been Counsel for the defence in Casement's Appeal (depicted addressing the Court to the right of the painting), wrote to the Lord Chancellor to ask if he could acquire the painting for the King's Inns in Dublin. It was decided that it was better to loan it, or as the Lord Chief Justice put it: 'We can adopt the suggestion of lending it to the King's Inns on indefinite loan which means we can forget to ask for its return.' Sullivan accepted, replying: 'Since even the profession have consigned the picture to gloom and forgetfulness for thirty years, I do not anticipate any new awakening to its charm. If such yearning shall seize the British Public they shall have it back. May you live and flourish as I would wish till then.'

Berlin, July, 2003

* For his help in writing the postscript, I would like to thank John McBratney, Honorary Secretary of King's Inns, Dublin. He was hitherto unknown to me, but happened to ring up Dorothy Cross as I sat with her on her lawn in Tully Cross, Connemara, where I had gone to stay on the second leg of the trip. He was excited to tell her he'd just been to London for the official unveiling (a small gathering of sixteen people) of *High Treason, Court of Criminal Appeal 1916: the Trial of Roger Casement* in the National Portrait Gallery: the very event I'd heard discussed on the radio my first morning in London.

---

[1] 'An Attempt at Restitution: A Memory of a German City', trans. Anthea Bell, *The New Yorker*, 20th and 27th December 2004.
[2] Rudyard Kipling, *Selected Poetry*, ed. Craig Raine, (London, Penguin Books: 1992), pp 101-2.
[3] Joseph Conrad, *Notes on Life and Letters*, The Cambridge Edition of The Works of Joseph Conrad, ed. J.H. Stape (Cambridge, Cambridge University Press: 2004), p 171.

Ali Smith

*

Loosed in Translation

The concept of translation turns up very physically near the end of the novel *Austerlitz* when Austerlitz visits the museum of veterinary medicine in Paris and comes across the exhibit of a flayed horseman by Honoré Fragonard, a man 'moved by a desire', says Austerlitz, 'to secure for the frail body at least some semblance of eternal life through a process of vitrification, by translating its so readily corruptible substance into a miracle of pure glass'.[1] A man becomes a window to himself. It's shortly after this that Austerlitz suffers another breakdown; these states always take the form of a breakdown of language, for this is a novel whose images of a tower-of-babel madness of noise and incomprehension are up against silence, whose power is the threshold to an equal madness.

Translation, in *The Emigrants,* is what Paul Bereyter, the beloved and wrongly-used teacher, teaches the boys is the most natural facility in the world, a thing of sunlit properties: 'one May morning we sat outside in the school yard, and on that fresh bright day we easily grasped what un beau jour meant, and that a chestnut tree in blossom might just as well be called un chataignier en fleurs'.[2] But the concept of words and their naming provides a slippage between naive hope and real despair throughout Sebald's work; in, for instance, Austerlitz's inability, at the moment of being told his real name, to connect the signifier with the signified or the word with anything meaningful at all;[3] or in *The Emigrants*, where, on a visit to Bad Kissingen's Jewish cemetery the narrator, considering the names of the dead, decides that 'perhaps there was nothing the Germans begrudged the Jews so much as their beautiful names, so intimately bound up with the country they lived in and with its language';[4] and right at the start of Sebald's literary oeuvre in the long, implacable, apocalyptic poem *After Nature* where Steller the explorer '…walks the paths / between the flowerbeds, marvels at the hothouses, filled with tropical plants / learns one new name after another / and is almost beside himself / with so much hope'.[5] Not long after he does, when he's hounded, arrested, left ill and ruined because he's complained to the authorities about their maltreatment of the indigenous peoples in the province in which he's been happily describing, classifying and drawing, Steller will finally 'wholly [grasp] the difference between nature and society'.[6] There is fierce anger in Sebald from the start, about the ways in which peoples and individuals are treated and ruined by what might be called mundane historical horror, by the systems called authority.

If words and the letters that make them up, or language in its written form, offer a kind of hope or order, it's revealed as a false one in *Vertigo*, where a small bilingual phrasebook which belonged to the narrator's great uncle becomes the narrator's travelling companion at the expense of his making any real connection with the two women in the same compartment as him on the train to Milan, and in which phrasebook 'everything seemed arranged in the best of all possible ways, quite as though the world was made up purely of letters and words and as if, through this act of transformation, even the greatest of horrors were safely banished, as if to each dark side there were a redeeming counterpart, to every evil its good, to every pain its pleasure, and to every lie a measure of truth'.[7] Sebald signals the sweet naivety in this, the attraction to the simplicity and cleanness of its 'act of transformation'. But everything Sebald writes can be said to be an attempt to reconcile this Jekyll and Hyde split state into something less absolute or divisive.

'All, all is language, even the reader,'[8] Christine Brooke-Rose puts it, and I think Sebald agrees. But if language and voice feature so very literally in this work, then silence is also a language, a voice, in it. From the dizzy-making fearful Svankmajer silence, of objects in an attic in *Vertigo*, as if 'this entire assemblage of the most diverse objects had been moving, in some sort of secret evolution, until the moment we entered',[9] to silence as memorial, the 'silent lament' of

Giotto's angels 'above our endless calamities for nigh on seven centuries',[10] Sebald is drawn to the word 'muted', declares in an interview his comfort with dust as substance, 'a sign of silence, somehow ... if I get into a house where the dust has been allowed to settle, I find that comforting'.[11] Perhaps this explains the surface antiquity of his narrative voice, a voice which couldn't be further from the wipe-clean soundbite culture we inhabit; explains what Michael Hofmann calls his 'insouciantly, provocatively grandiloquent'[12] manner, redolent with ledgy subclauses which knowingly slow the pace of thought. But if this is grandiloquence, then it's an unexpected grandiloquence, from the margins, geographically and emotionally.

So: what gets lost, what gets found, what gets loosed, freed, liberated in the work of Sebald? The literal getting-lost of the narrator, either in his ramblings, or his mental paralysis as he waits at another station or lies on another hotel bed, is practically a Sebaldian trope; typically here in *The Rings of Saturn*, in post-Troubles Ireland, where he's taking bed-and-breakfast in the decay of an old aristocratic architectural pile: 'Whenever I rested on that bed over the next few days, my consciousness began to dissolve at the edges, so that at times I could hardly have said how I had got there or indeed where I was'.[13] This repeating lostness, with its veils and mists and fogs and bewilderment, is a posturing, but one that's empathetic with all human blindnesses, one that actually postures absence, in the same way as his grandiloquence postures marginality; this is enervation as dandification, the paralysed flaneur at large in a landscape of all the world's (and history's) troubles.

It is useful to see this lostness in general philosophical terms, what George Steiner (in his *Antigones*) calls 'the Hegelian intuition of a lost at-homeness in existence, of a necessary voyage through alienation and self-division ... [where] self-exile seems implicit in the life of consciousness, in the capacities of the human ego to think "outside" and "against" itself'.[14] But Sebald's narratorial exile is both psychological and literal, both personal romance and political/philosophical positioning, an argument for the sake and the consequence of something larger than the self. His prose is a thinking peripatetic, one in honour, you might say, of Benjamin, following, on foot, 'the marks of pain which ... trace countless fine lines' in what's left of the century which destroyed Benjamin.[15] His getting lost leads into and out of itself in a new version of quest.

Lost in the maze at Somerleyton, his narrator arrives, as it were, at the wartime memories of a gardener he meets, William Hazel, who remembers watching the airwar aircraft setting off to carpet-bomb Germany, in fact can't forget the sight, sees it again 'whenever I close my eyes, to this day', and remembers too, as Sebald does in his lectures *On The Natural History of Destruction*, the loss, the blanking, the silencing, in German consciousness, of that literal occurrence: 'I even learnt German, after a fashion, so that I could read what the Germans themselves had said about the bombings. ... No one at the time seemed to have written about their experiences ... Even if you asked people directly, it was as if everything had been erased from their minds.'[16] Later in the book, losing himself again, this time in the Borges/Lear 'labyrinth of the heath', he finds himself finally at his friend the poet and translator Michael Hamburger's house, where he relates, in first person, Hamburger's own exile, his return to his childhood, to Berlin, and the culmination of blanks and losses as he stands at the door of the building he'd once lived in and, caught in a sick and bewilderingly simple-seeming puzzlement, can't solve it, can't change what's happened in the past, can't go back in.[17]

Melancholia be damned: in any close examination of the workings of his fiction, Sebald's is an inquiry into despair which produces a tightrope-balanced negotiation between the workings of the mind and the state of being out of your mind. His art proliferates with asylums, with the assertion that 'mental suffering is effectively without end',[18] in a literature that's an inquiry into the relationship between health and writing, between the body and the book. Its visions of the real, recognizably mappable world are despairing. London's taxi-ranks are literally underlaid with the dead;[19] and if this is an ancestor-echo of the way that Conrad, after *The Secret Agent*, at the last turn of the century, saw London as a city dark 'enough to bury five millions of lives',[20] then Sebald's vision of Paris's new library, his Resnais-like revelation of the dehumanising administrative systematic hell of the metropolis of books[21] (which can't fail to call up the Resnais film he doesn't mention, 'Night and Fog',[22] which redolates nevertheless through his earlier descriptions of Theresienstadt), his vision of the foundation of reading, built on shared theft and guilt, the Fascist looting from the Parisian Jews, is a meld of revelation and despair all his own. His work addresses what he calls, in the preface to *On The Natural History of Destruction*, 'the looking and looking away at the same time'.[23] He works with the opening of the eyes, and the opening of the I, the open first person; he brings us up so close to our own blindnesses, blanks and ignorances that we see again, and in the vitality of this seeing, in its merging with an all-ends-in-death lugubriousness, there's a contradiction. The closing pages of *The Rings of Saturn* fuse virtuosity and despair into a new knowing, a new literary expression of pain and, yes, pleasure; against all the odds, all the evidence, somehow the knowledge of the interconnectings in the crescendo of despair is also consolation.

As Sebald put it to Eleanor Wachtel in an interview, 'tragedy is still a pattern of order and an attempt to give meaning to something, to a life or to a series of lives. It's still, as it were, a positive way of looking at things.'[24] I imagine him with his mournful demeanour firmly on, telling Wachtel, 'if you imagine the amount of painkillers that are consumed, say, in the city of New York every year, you might be able to make a mountain out of it on which you could go ski-ing'. [25] The late Roger Deakin identified not just the naturalist in Sebald but also the duality in his work where the 'bass-line of profound anxiety, like the elephants in Forster's description of Beethoven's 5th symphony in *Howards End*, a kind of silent scream like Munch's', sits alongside a much less celebrated puckishness, Sebald as Robin Goodfellow, the 'genius' of whose work is that it can put the girdle round the earth in forty minutes, 'take us effortlessly wherever he wants in time or place, without the need of narrative sense'.[26]

And though he's not exactly Sid James (though there is an arguably curmudgeonly connection somewhere there, for in true Sebaldian terms nothing is not connected), Sebald is often funny, with a surrealist's caprice; for instance when the narrator in his giddiest book, *Vertigo*, finds himself on a bus in Italy fascinated by how much two sniggering twins resemble the young Kafka, and, since he has no camera and the novel is all about forms of evidence, starts trying to explain the resemblance to the boys' parents; when he asks if they'll send him a photo of their boys to his English address, *Metamorphosis* meets *Death in Venice*; something funny lines the underside of uncomfortable, and vice versa.[27]

The photographs carefully placed through his work are a source of evidence and absence at once, the evidence of a world where silence ends up saying more than words. In *The Emigrants* what takes the place of language under the force of the 'thickening silence' felt by Max Ferber's parents, Jews under the first pressure of increasing persecution, is cinema: his father going 'to the cinema more and more often, to see cowboy films and the mountaineering films of Luis Trenker'.[28]

There must be hundreds of thesis papers about the screen in Sebald's work, and about Sebald and Freud and screen memory, repressed elements, our defence against them. But for me the most telling moment, when it comes to notions of image and meaning in Sebald's work, occurs in *Austerlitz*, when Austerlitz, a fictional character desperate in a search for an image of his lost mother, a fictional character, tries to track down a surviving copy of the real propaganda film of Theresienstadt, made by the Nazis, a film in which the concentration camp, in the most gruesome of ironies, performs a version of itself as a pleasant holiday spa. What happens is that Austerlitz finds himself helplessly caught up, as it were, in the act. 'I kept thinking that if only the film could be found I might perhaps be able to see or gain some inkling of what it was really like, and then I imagined recognizing Agata beyond any possibility of doubt... perhaps among the guests outside the fake coffee-house, or ... among a group of ghetto residents out for a stroll ... until at last I thought I could sense her stepping out of the frame and passing over into me'. He finds a copy of the film, watches it and can see nothing; he slows it down so that fifteen minutes in Theresienstadt now lasts an hour. He sees a woman in the shadow of a moment, and convinces himself she might well be Agata. The real still of a real woman from the real film is reproduced in the novel. As soon as Austerlitz shows Vera, the fictional character who knew his mother, she verifies: it's not Agata. Then inserted into the text there's another photo, from elsewhere, of someone who, apparently, 'really is' Agata.[29]

The disturbingness of the terrible paucity revealed by this incident almost rivals the disturbingness of the Nazi experiment, and this is a purposeful revelation. The real loss, left as silence by Sebald, comes in the dismissal of the real woman, whoever she was, in the slowed-down, 'found' image of Theresienstadt, a woman first someone, then no-one. If she's not Agata, then who is she? The real tragedy here, unmentioned, slipping past almost unregistered, is this woman's. Where history made her nobody, narrative plot has first singled her out and then made her a nobody all over again.

Though this slowing-down of the propaganda machine to reveal the real weight and distortion of the Nazi vision must also have been influenced by Douglas Gordon's 1993 installation, '24-Hour Psycho',[30] I've often wondered whether Sebald, who latterly taught film studies, for whom film features largely in his prose fictions, and who writes about film piercingly and often in the essays he wrote throughout his career, knew the work of structuralist New York experimental filmmaker, Ken Jacobs, for instance his 1969 version of a 1905 Mutoscope 'Tom Tom The Piper's Son',[31] where early film footage is stretched and slowed and stilled and speeded up by what Jacobs calls his 'Nazi combat camera' until fragments reveal both realism and abstraction, and the co-ordinates of how we see things are, at some points physically painfully, undone. 'Get lost,' Ken Jacobs says is his advice to his film students. 'And get lost again.'[32]

What's found in Sebald is often the twinned opposite, the language in the silence and the silence in the language, the blind in the sight and the sight in the blind, the doubleness in the bind. Railway stations are 'places marked by both blissful happiness and profound misfortune'.[33] 'The fact is, in Sebald nobody is ever about,' Alan Bennett wrote;[34] all the same, quite mysteriously for such works of evident solitudinous captivation, Sebald's work is simultaneously heavily peopled, full of voices, multilogues, endlessly surprising meetings with strangers and friends and the dead and the gone lives of various people, all wandering at large. Sebald's working process, an avowal of randomness and plotlessness, provides a sensual revelation of the living shape of things, or the plot right under the nose: 'you find odd details which lead you somewhere else', he said in interview, 'and so it's a form of unsystematic searching … in the same way in which, say, a dog runs through a field. If you look at a dog following the advice of his nose, he traverses a patch of ground in a completely unplottable manner. And he invariably finds what he's looking for: ... I've always had dogs, I've learned from them how to do this.'[35]

When Sebald said this, in interview in New York in 2001, the audience laughed. But it's typical of Sebald, a celebrator of creatures, birds, moths, butterflies, trees, the beyond-human, a man who presents the planet itself as a silently vociferous character in his work, to translate the self in this way. Compare, too, the freedom of the dog in this analogy with repeated images in his work of incarcerated creatures, in their uncomprehending state in zoos and cages. Sebald, again echoing Woolf, both hymns and fears 'the murmur/ of the millionfold proliferating molluscs/ woodlice and leeches"; [36] he places it alongside the hugeness of the erosive violence of nature itself, held as an equal force of destruction alongside imperialism in *The Rings of Saturn*, a force just as capable of tightening, noose-like, around us.

Sebald positions us precariously, in the slight slippage between a word like noose and one like nose; the narrator following his nose, pervasively on the scent of coincidence in a kind of loitering with intent. Sebald was intent on the co- of coincidence, the aspect of things coming unexpectedly together. The lack of parenthesis through his writing, and what might be called a reluctance about paragraphs, textually signal a writer uninterested in dividing. Consider his interest, too, in the non-identifiable nature of his own writing, the openness of its form. Consider the open or composite narrator who develops over the course of the fictions, and the open or composite writer too, who makes a feature of other people's work in the window his own work provides. 'And I remember, Vera told me, said Austerlitz...'[37] The pivotal formal device in *Austerlitz* is that of narrator contained by narrator contained by narrator, with the closedness and disclosure of a set of Russian dolls, or is it the opening outward of rings on the surface of water, or both? *Austerlitz* is a tale told at a remove at exactly the same time as one told at an intimacy the level of which forms and changes the nature of the narratorial self. It's an art of storytelling in which reported speech becomes a kind of enfolding, a state of inclusion as intimate as breath pattern. In Sebald's writing what gets found, and simultaneously analysed, is a force of interconnection.

In *Vertigo*, the narrator draws attention to the democracy in a work by Pisanello, 'in which every feature, the principals and the extras alike, the birds in the sky, the green forest and every single leaf of it, are all granted an equal and undiminished right to exist'.[38] Art in Sebald tends to stand both outside and in time, rather like the tree outside Max Ferber's studio in the Manchester wastelands of *The Emigrants* is always in blossom.[39] Sebald can't look away, himself, from the lived lives of artists and writers, especially their earlier lives, which can be said to have formed them as artists. But more, to quote from his chapter on Stendhal in *Vertigo*: 'what is it that undoes a writer?'[40]

Undoes as in ruins, or takes apart? Or undoes as in loosens, or frees, or liberates? Both. The first prison image in Sebald's literary work turns up directly after an image of the blind having their sight restored in *After Nature*, when Sebald's autobiographical narrator goes walking around Manchester on a Sunday looking for Strangeways prison, and instead finds himself 'in a sort of no-man's land', in what's left of Manchester's Jewish district.[41] *Vertigo's* first prisoner (after a very wild dog – and animals in incarceration in Sebald's work are revelatory about the treatment of all living things) is Casanova, writer and lover, flung into the attic dungeons of the Doge's Palace in Venice because he's the kind of person 'their Excellencies' have decided to remove from society. He escapes, by means of the 'law' of coincidence, by finding himself and a future in 'a seemingly random operation of words and numbers'.[42]

Freedom, however, involves great loss. Max Ferber, the artist in *The Emigrants*, recalls his arrival in England and the strange freedom of settling in at a foreign school, so that 'it grew steadily harder for me to write my letters home or to read the letters that arrived from home every fortnight ... when the letters stopped coming, in November 1941, I was relieved at first'. Freedom is a state of naivety. 'Only gradually did it dawn on me that I would never again be able to write home.'[43] It's also a tortuous business in itself; as Aunt Fini, commenting on Ambros Adelwarth in the same work, suggests: 'telling stories was as much a torment to him as an attempt at self-liberation. He was at once saving himself, in some way, and mercilessly destroying himself.'[44]

At one point in *The Emigrants* the words gaol and oubliette are interchangeable.⁴⁵ Hotel rooms rattle their keys throughout Sebald's writing; open doors and windows are a kind of architectural dream of freedom, or a terrible charade of hope, as when the 'friendly happy folk who had been spared the horrors of war' look out of the windows of Theresienstadt's buildings at the Red Cross officials being hoodwinked by the Nazi charade near the end of the very long sentence in *Austerlitz*,⁴⁶ a book whose beginning opens on one of Sebald's repeated analogies, the notion that fortifications built to keep people safe generally end up imprisoning them.⁴⁷

To focus for a moment on the horrific connectivity of that eleven-page-long sentence, on the doggedness of its refutal of all literary naiveties about the glory of connectivity: it leaves a phrase like Forster's 'only connect' hanging ragged, or, rather, cancels the phrase's naivety and rewrites its urgency in the new light, the new dark, of the end of the twentieth century; reveals *Austerlitz* as a taking to task of literary mode. 'The long long sentence in *Austerlitz* about the busily deranged activities of the Nazi authorities at Theresienstadt,' Anthea Bell says, 'I always remember that when I was drafting that, I put a full stop after a couple of pages – and then knew at once I mustn't.' ⁴⁸ It is a relentless connectivity machine. It is strung between losses: its final phrase is 'lost without trace' and it begins directly after Austerlitz considers what gets lost in translation, commenting on the way German, the language, forces words together, compounds them to make new words – and then the sentence, in its ruthlessness, reveals the detainee sense of compound and compounds us as readers. It is stealthy, it creeps up on its reader in a build-up of panic and inexorability as it piles itself up on itself: at its centre is the revelation of the hecatomb of bodies waiting to be dealt with in the morgue. It keeps itself going like the crematorium 'kept going day and night in cycles of forty minutes at a time'. Its couple of anomalies are remarkable. It lightly, ironically, uncharacteristically uses the word 'medley' to describe the carts and hearses which shift the very heavy piles of dead around town; the effect of this word's strange lightness is as devastating as the use, later, of the first simile in the sentence, where the 40,145 prisoners who've been standing (ironically in comparative freedom, beyond the gate of the camp) for hours in the November cold and rain and dark, because the SS men have simply forgotten to dismiss their dawn roll-call, are seen as 'swaying like reeds in the showers that now swept over the countryside': and then it's as if language itself has loosed the obscenity of what might be called the grotesque simile which follows, when the Nazis make a concentration camp look like a spa.[49]

Up against this foul machine, what do we have? A visit to the old MOD site on Orford Ness, 'which resembled a penal colony in the Far East', leaves the narrator of *The Rings of Saturn* 'liberated', with all the loadedness the word has for a writer of Sebald's formation. 'It was as if I were passing through an undiscovered country, and I still remember that I felt, at the same time, both utterly liberated and deeply despondent. I had not a single thought in my head. With each step I took, the emptiness within and the emptiness without grew ever greater and the silence more profound.' Liberation here is a kind of death where the notion that no man is an island is disproved – until, that is, the narrator meets, in the long grass of the deserted military site, another living creature, a hare, terrified by the sight of him, 'a curiously human expression on its face that was rigid with terror and strangely divided', and which, when it finally leaps out of its 'paralysed state', frees him too, as 'with an undiminished clarity" he sees himself 'become one with it'.[50]

It's in these liminalities, in the space between lost and found, ruin and construction, imprisonment and liberation, blindness and seeing; it's in what moves, what shifts between states which seem as irreconcilable as fact and fiction, to reveal that nothing is divided, nothing is not connected for the good and the bad, and nothing can be designated alien to us, it's in the revelation of the flayed, displayed fragility of the self, the self both saved and destroyed, that Sebald's act of translation, or vision of cohesion, becomes a match for despair and potent beyond any cliché of hope.

❦

Reading Sebald in translation is, in many ways, the whole point. 'These questions carry me/ over the border,"[51] he writes in *After Nature*; throughout his work he questions the borders of country, nationality, language, identity, knowledge, art, reality. And what happens when things aren't 'translated into the spoken/ language of the present', he says, is that we're left with a 'broken corpus'.[52] In Sebald's writing, human beings, timeless, historic, broken, gone and alive, appear and move and speak above all through the agency of others.

If we think of translation as a skein of interconnectings made by people not machine, the very act of which resists the absolute, and in which, as Benjamin, in translation, puts it, 'the great motif of integrating many tongues into one true language is at work';[53] if we think of translation as a liminal state which admits the never-definitive, which moves between the original and the new, in the continuing refinement of language as a communal act, typical of the shared project that all writing is; if we admit the ways in which translation goes beyond the self, beyond the broken, beyond the fixed, beyond the only of connect and to the core of its nature, then we should all aspire to be read in translation, to exist in the between that translation is, in process, bigger than our selves, in the vital state between the words and their possible meanings, between language and all the possible languages.

[1] *Austerlitz*, p. 374.
[2] *The Emigrants*, p.38.
[3] *Austerlitz*, p.94.
[4] *The Emigrants*, p.224.
[5] *After Nature*, p.49.
[6] *After Nature*, p.73.
[7] *Vertigo*, p.105.
[8] Christine Brook-Rose 'Whatever Happened to Narratology?' *Poetics Today* special issue Narratology Revisited I , Vol. 11, No. 2 (Summer, 1990), pp.283-293; p.290.
[9] *Vertigo*, p.224.
[10] *Vertigo*, p.84.
[11] Sebald in conversation with Eleanor Wachtel in 'Ghost Hunter'. *The Emergence of Memory: Conversations with W.G. Sebald*. Ed. Lynne Sharon Swartz (New York, Seven Stories: 2007), pp.37-62; pp.58-9.

¹² Michael Hofmann 'A Chilly Extravagance' *The Emergence of Memory*, pp.87-92; p.89.
¹³ *The Rings of Saturn*, p. 210.
¹⁴ George Steiner *Antigones* (New Haven, Yale UP: 1996), p.15.
¹⁵ *Austerlitz*, p.16.
¹⁶ *The Rings of Saturn*, p.39.
¹⁷ *The Rings of Saturn*, pp.175-8.
¹⁸ *The Emigrants*, p.170.
¹⁹ *Austerlitz*, p.184.
²⁰ Joseph Conrad 'Author's Note' *The Secret Agent* (London, Penguin: 2007), pp.247-55; p.250. First published 1907.
²¹ *Austerlitz*, p.364.
²² 'Night and Fog'. Dir. Alain Resnais (Argos, 1955).
²³ *On The Natural History of Destruction*, p. ix.
²⁴ 'Ghost Hunter', p. 58.
²⁵ "Ghost Hunter", pp. 55-6.
²⁶ Roger Deakin 'The Fearless Digressions of Sebald/ Introducing Sebald' *Five Dials No. 5*. Ed. Craig Taylor (Hamish Hamilton, 2008) [online] http://fivedials.com/files/fivedials_no5.pdf accessed 18 July 2013, p.14.
²⁷ *Vertigo*, pp.88-90.
²⁸ *The Emigrants*, p.185. Trenker was later an inspiration to the Nazi genius of the propaganda image, Leni Riefenstahl.
²⁹ *Austerlitz*, pp.342-54.
³⁰ Douglas Gordon '24 Hour Psycho', (1993) Film installation. First screened in Glasgow & Berlin.
³¹ 'Tom, Tom the Pipers Son', Dir. Ken Jacobs (LFMC 1969)
³² Ken Jacobs 'Beating my Tom, Tom', *Exploding* special issue on 'Tom, Tom the Pipers Son' (October 2000), p.5.
³³ *Austerlitz*, p.45.
³⁴ Alan Bennett *Untold Stories* (London, Faber: 2005), pp.308-9.
³⁵ Sebald in conversation with Joseph Cuomo in 'A Conversation with W.G. Sebald' *The Emergence of Memory*, pp.93-118; p.94.
³⁶ *After Nature*, p.110.
³⁷ *Austerlitz*, p.226.
³⁸ *Vertigo*, p.73.
³⁹ *The Emigrants*, p.160 and p. 179.
⁴⁰ *Vertigo*, p.15.
⁴¹ *After Nature*, pp.98-9.
⁴² *Vertigo*, pp.56-9.
⁴³ *The Emigrants*, pp.190-1.
⁴⁴ *The Emigrants*, p.100.
⁴⁵ *The Emigrants*, p.178.
⁴⁶ *Austerlitz*, p.341.
⁴⁷ *Austerlitz*, pp. 16-24.
⁴⁸ E-mail interview and correspondence between Anthea Bell and the author, December 2010.
⁴⁹ *Austerlitz*, pp.331-42.
⁵⁰ *The Rings of Saturn*, pp.233-5.
⁵¹ *After Nature*, p.104.
⁵² *After Nature*, p.88.

J.M. Coetzee

*

W.G. Sebald, After Nature

W.G. Sebald was born in 1944 in the corner of southern Germany where Germany, Austria and Switzerland converge. In his early twenties he travelled to England to further his studies in German literature, and spent most of his working life teaching in England at a provincial university. By the time of his death in 2001 he had a solid body of academic publication to his name, mainly on the literature of Austria.

But in his middle years Sebald also blossomed as a writer, first with a book of poetry, then with a sequence of four prose fictions. The second of these, *The Emigrants*, brought him wide attention, particularly in the English-speaking world, where its blend of storytelling, fictive biography, antiquarian essay, dream and philosophical rumination, executed in elegant if rather lugubrious prose and supplemented with photographic documentation of endearingly amateurish quality, struck a decidedly new note (the German public was accustomed by this time to the crossing and indeed trampling of boundaries between fiction and nonfiction).

The people in Sebald's books are for the most part what used to be called melancholics. The tone of their lives is defined by a hard-to-articulate sense that they do not belong in the world, that perhaps human beings in general do not belong here. They are humble enough not to claim they are preternaturally sensitive to the currents of history – in fact they tend to believe there is something wrong with them – but the tenor of Sebald's enterprise is to suggest that his people are prophetic, even though the fate of the prophet in the modern world is to be obscure and unheard.

What is the basis of their melancholy? Again and again Sebald suggests they are labouring under the burden of Europe's recent history, a history in which the Holocaust looms large. Internally they are racked by conflict between a self-protective urge to block off a painful past and a blind groping for something, they know not what, that has been lost.

Although in Sebald's stories the overcoming of amnesia is often figured as the culmination of a labour of research – burrowing in archives, tracking down witnesses – the recovery of the past only confirms what at the deepest level his people already know, as their steady melancholy in the face of the world already expresses, and as, in their intermittent breakdowns or catalepsies, their bodies have all along been saying in their own language, the language of symptom: that there is no cure, no salvation.

The form that the crisis in melancholy in Sebald takes is well defined. There is a lead-up full of compulsive activity, often consisting of nocturnal walking, dominated by feelings of apprehension. The world seems full of messages in some secret code. Dreams come thick and fast. Then there is the experience itself: one is on a cliff or in an aircraft, looking down in space but also back in time; man and his activities seem tiny to the point of insignificance; all sense of purpose dissolves. The vision precipitates a kind of swoon in which the mind collapses.

Vertigo, Sebald's first long prose work, emphasizes the apocalyptic dimension of this mental crisis. In the final section of the book the 'I' narrator takes a trip to his birthplace, the town of W. There, as he pores over a clutter of objects in a dusty attic, a flood of memories is released, followed by intimations that retribution is about to be visited on the town. Fearing madness, he flees. The homeward trip through southern Germany is eerie. The landscape has an alien air; people at the train station look like refugees from doomed cities; before his eyes someone reads a book that, as his later bibliographical researches prove, does not exist.[1]

In Sebald, 1914 often appears as the year when Europe took the wrong turn. But, looked at more closely, the pre-1914 idyll reveals itself to be without foundation. Did the true wrong turn take place earlier, then, with the triumph of Enlightenment reason and the enthronement of the idea of progress? While there is plenty of historical awareness in Sebald – the cities and landscapes through which people move are ghost-ridden, layered with signs of the past – and while part of his general gloom is about the destruction of habitat in the name of progress, he is not conservative in the sense of harking back to a golden age when mankind was at home in the world in a good, natural way. On the contrary he subjects the concept of home and being at home to a continual sceptical scrutiny. One of his literary-critical books is a study of the notion of *Heimat* (homeland) in Austrian literature. Playing on the ambiguity of the word *unheimlich* (unhomelike, unfamiliar, hence uncanny), he suggest that for today's Austrians, citizens of a notional country whose territory and population have altered with each turn in modern European history, there ought to be something ghostly in feeling at home.[2]

The Rings of Saturn comes the closest amongst Sebald's books to what we usually think of as nonfiction. It is written to tame the 'paralyzing horror' that overtakes its author – that is to say its 'I' figure – in the face of the decline of the eastern region of England and the destruction of its landscape. (Of course the 'I' in Sebald's books is not to be identified with the historical W.G. Sebald. Nevertheless, Sebald as author plays mischievously with similarities between the two, to the point of reproducing snapshots and passport photographs of 'Sebald' in his texts.)

After a walking tour through the region, Sebald or 'I' is hospitalised in a cataleptic state, with symptoms that include a sense of utter alienation linked to hallucinations of being in a high place looking down on the world. To this vertigo he gives a metaphysical rather than a merely psychological interpretation. 'If we view ourselves from a great height,' he says, ' it is frightening to realise how little we know about our species, our purpose and our end.' A spinning of the mind followed by mental collapse is what happens when we see ourselves from God's point of view.[3]

Sebald did not call himself a novelist – prose writer was the term he preferred – but his enterprise nevertheless depends for its success on attaining lift-off from the biographical or the essayistic – the prosaic in the everyday sense of the word – into the realm of the imaginative. The mysterious ease with which he is able to achieve such lift-off is the clearest proof of his genius. But *The Rings of Saturn* does not always succeed in this respect. Chapters on Joseph Conrad, Roger Casement, the poet Edward Fitzgerald, and the last empress of China, all of whom – surprisingly – have links with East Anglia, remain anchored in the prosaic.

In the earlier books the subject of time is not treated in any depth, perhaps because Sebald is not sure his medium will bear the weight of too much philosophising. When the subject is broached, it tends to be via references to the idealist paradoxes of Jorge Luis Borges, or, in *The Rings of Saturn*, to one of Borges's mentors, the neo-Platonist Sir Thomas Browne. But in *Austerlitz* (2001), Sebald's most ambitious book, time is confronted full on.

Time has no real existence, asserts Jacques Austerlitz, a professor of European art and architecture who lost his past when his Jewish parents packed him off to England as a small child to escape the coming catastrophe. Instead of the common medium of time, says Austerlitz, there exist interconnected pockets of space-time whose topology we may never understand, but between which the so-called living and the so-called dead can travel and thus meet one another.[4] A snapshot, he goes on, is a kind of eye or node of linkage between past and present, enabling the living to see the dead and the dead to see the living, the survivors. (This denial of the reality of time provides a retrospective rationale for the photographs that pepper Sebald's prose texts.)

One consequence of the denial of time is that the past is reduced to a set of interlocking memories in the minds of the living. Austerlitz is haunted by the knowledge that each day a quantum of the past, including his own past, vanishes as people die and memories are extinguished. Here he echoes the anxiety expressed by Rainer Maria Rilke in his letters about the duty of the artist as a bearer of cultural memory. Indeed, behind Sebald's scholar hero, so out of place in the late twentieth century, loom several dead masters from the last years of Hapsburg Austria: Rilke, the Hugo von Hofmannsthal of the 'Letter to Lord Chandos', Kafka, Wittgenstein.

Shortly before his death Sebald published a book of poems with images by the artist Tess Jaray.[5] It is a work of no great ambition, suggesting that verse-writing was a mere hobby for him. Yet his first book of poetry, *Nach der Natur* (1988), translated as *After Nature*, is a work of considerable scope. Though its imagery is more challenging than anything in Sebald's prose works, the verse retains the Sebaldian virtues of rhetorical elegance and clarity, and sits well in English translation, as indeed does everything he wrote.

After Nature is made up of three long poems. The first is about Mathias Grünewald, the sixteenth-century painter, whose life story Sebald cobbles together from scanty historical sources and observations on his paintings. Chief amongst the paintings is the altarpiece Grünewald executed for the Antonine monastery of Isenheim in Alsace, in his time the home of a hospital for plagues of various kinds. In the darkest of the Isenheim paintings – the temptation of St. Anthony, the crucifixion and deposition of Jesus – Sebald's Grünewald sees creation as a field of experiment for blind, amoral natural forces, one of nature's crazier productions being the human mind itself, capable not only of mimicking its creator and inventing ingenious methods of destruction, but of tormenting itself – as in the case of Grünewald – with visions of the insanity of life.

Equally bleak is Grünewald's *Crucifixion* in Basel, where the strange, murky lighting creates an effect of time rushing backward. Behind the painting, Sebald suggests, lie premonitions of apocalypse stemming from an eclipse of the sun in central Europe in 1502, a 'secret sickening away of the world,/ in which a phantasmal encroachment of dusk/ in the midst of daytime like a fainting fit/ poured through the vault of the sky.'[6]

The darkness of Grünewald's vision is not just a matter of an idiosyncratically melancholy temperament. Via connections with the messianic prophet Thomas Münzer, Grünewald knew and responded to the horrors of the Thirty Years War, which included a widespread atrocity any artist would shudder at, the gouging out of eyes; furthermore, through his wife, a convert born in the Frankfurt ghetto, he has an intimate experience of the persecution of Europe's Jews.

The coda of this first poem consists of a single image: the world overtaken by a new ice age, white and lifeless, which is all that the eye sees when the optic nerve is torn.

The second of the *After Nature* poems is again about vastness and blankness and iciness. Its hero, Georg Wilhelm Steller (1709-1746), is a child of the Enlightenment, a young German intellectual who has abandoned theology to study natural science. In pursuit of his ambition of cataloguing the fauna and flora of the frozen north, Steller travels to St. Petersburg, a city that looms like a phantom out of the 'future's resounding emptiness', where he joins the expedition led by Vitus Bering to map the sea passage from Russia's Arctic ports to the Pacific.[7]

The expedition is successful. Steller even sets foot for a few brief hours on the North American land mass. On the way back to Russia, however, the voyagers suffer shipwreck. The melancholy Bering dies; the survivors make their way home in a makeshift craft, all but Steller, who goes off into the Siberian interior to collect specimens and familiarise himself with the native peoples. There he too dies, leaving behind a list of plants and a manuscript destined to become a guidebook for hunters and trappers.

The aims of the Grünewald and the Steller poems are not biographical or historical in the ordinary sense. Though the scholarship behind them is thorough – Sebald had publications on art-historical subjects to his name; he clearly did his homework on the Bering expedition – scholarship takes second place to what he intuits about his subjects and perhaps projects upon them (this may give a clue as to how Sebald constructed characters in his later prose fictions). Instance one: his claim that Grünewald, though married, was secretly homosexual, involved for many years in 'a male friendship wavering/ between horror and loyalty' with a fellow painter named Matthis Nithart, is, among specialists, highly contentious: 'Matthis Nithart' may simply be Grünewald's own baptismal name. Instance two: the historical Steller appears to have been a vain and supercilious young man, interested mainly in making a name for himself, who met his death when he fell into a drunken stupor in sub-zero temperatures.[8] None of this is in Sebald.

It is thus best to think of Grünewald and Steller as personae, masks that enable Sebald to project back into the past a character type, ill at ease in the world, indeed in exile from it, that may be his own but that he feels possesses a certain genealogy which his reading and researches uncover. The Grünewald persona, with his Manichean view of the creation, is more fully worked out than the Steller persona, which is little more than a set of gestures, perhaps because Sebald could find – or create – no believable depths to his character.

'Dark Night Sallies Forth', the third of the poems in *After Nature*, is more overtly autobiographical. Here Sebald, as 'I', takes stock of himself as an individual but also as inheritor of Germany's recent history. In images and fragments of narrative, the poem tells his story from his birth in 1944 under the sign of Saturn, the cold planet, to the 1980s. Some of the images – we are familiar with the practice by now from Sebald's prose fictions – come from Europe's cultural treasure chest, in this case two paintings by Albrecht Altdorfer (1480-1538): of the destruction of Sodom; and of the battle of Arbela, fought between Alexander of Macedon and Darius, king of Persia.

Seeing the Sodom painting for the first time precipitates a *déjà vu* experience, which Sebald connects with the bombing of German cities in World War II and the refusal of his parents to speak about the subject. The general willed amnesia of his parents' generation, the chief source of his grievance against and alienation from them, forces him to do their remembering for them. (Putting an end to this spell of historical amnesia became a matter of gathering national concern in Germany at the turn of the century. It is the theme of Sebald's own *Luftkrieg und Literatur*, 1999, translated as *On The Natural History of Destruction*.)

In the poem the spectacle of destruction of Sodom leads to a personal crisis ('I nearly went out of my mind'), which Sebald links to his recurrent episodes of vertigo. With hindsight we can see that it will also lead to the labour of reparation constituted by his four prose works, and particularly by his biographies of Jews, both imaginary (the people in *The Emigrants; Austerlitz*) and real (his friend and now his translator Michael Hamburger in *The Rings of Saturn*).[9]

The most clearly narrative section of *After Nature*, written with a nod in the direction of *The Prelude*, William Wordsworth's poem about his formative years, tells the story of Sebald's sojourn in the Manchester of the 1960s, a city in which early industrial Europe survives into the late twentieth century as a kind of necropolis or kingdom of the dead ('These images/ often plunged me into a quasi/ sublunary state of deep/ melancholia').[10]

The East Anglian landscape where Sebald later finds himself is equally bleak: farms have been replaced with asylums or prisons or homes for the aged or testing ranges for weapons. Nor is modern England unique on its ugliness. Flying over Germany, he has another of his darkly visionary experiences.

> Cities phosphorescent
> on the riverbank, industry's
> glowing piles waiting
> beneath the smoke trails
> like ocean giants for the siren's
> blare, the twitching lights
> of rail- and motorways, the murmur
> of the millionfold proliferating molluscs,
> wood lice and leeches, cold putrefaction,
> the groans and the rocky ribs,
> the mercury shine, the clouds that
> chased through the towers of Frankfurt,
> time stretched out and time speeded up,
> all this raced through my mind
> and was already so near the end
> that every breath of air made my
> face shudder.[11]

Visions like this lead him to think of himself as Icarus, the boy who, sailing high above the earth with homemade wings, sees what no ordinary mortal is allowed to see. When he falls, as he is doomed to do, will anyone pay attention or, as in Brueghel's famous painting, will the world simply go on with its business?

Vertigo points him backward to his childhood problems with keeping his balance, and forward to the second Altdorfer painting, *The Battle of Arbela*, a panorama of slaughter on a huge scale rendered in detail of hallucinatory, vertigo-inducing minuteness. The painting ought to precipitate another of his melancholic collapses. Instead it leads to a rather unconvincing transcendence with which the poem ends: an opening out of vision beyond horizons of unending warfare, East versus West, to a new future:

> ... still further in the distance,
> towering up in the dwindling light,
> the mountain ranges,
> snow-covered and ice-bound,
> of the strange, unexplored,
> African continent. [12]

After Nature has its dead patches and moments of empty portentousness, but in all it is a work of great power and seriousness fully worthy to stand beside the prose works of Sebald's last decade.

---

[1] *Vertigo*, pp 171-263.
[2] *Unheimliche Heimat: Essays zur osterreichischen Literatur* (Salzburg & Wien, Rezidenz:1991)
[3] *The Rings of Saturn*, p 92.
[4] *Austerlitz*, p 261.
[5] *For Years Now* (London, Short Books: 2001)
[6] *After Nature*, p 30.
[7] *After Nature*, p 48.
[8] *After Nature*, p 19.
[9] *After Nature*, p 19.
[10] *After Nature*, p 97.
[11] *After Nature*, pp 109-10.
[12] *After Nature*, p112-13.

Will Self

*

Absent Jews and Invisible Executioners

I have been asked if I was aware of the moral implications of what I was doing. As I told the tribunal at Nuremberg, I did not know that Hitler was a Nazi. The truth was that for years I thought he worked for the phone company. When I did finally find out what a monster he was, it was too late to do anything as I had already made a down payment on some furniture. Once, towards the end of the war I did contemplate loosening the Fuhrer's neck napkin and allowing a few tiny hairs to get down his back, but at the last minute my nerve failed me. [1]

Following Freud – himself an exile, driven out by the Nazis – there are some things too serious not to joke about – and this applies to Hitler, to the vile regime he initiated, and even to the murders – through aggressive war, through mass shootings, extermination camps and forced marches – that this regime enacted. Mass murders the true extent of which will never now be established with complete accuracy – twenty million, thirty? What can such figures tell us, how can they convey the sentience of a single individual crushed beneath the Nazis' juggernaut, let alone a myriad of such lived nightmares?

I should qualify the above: some things are too serious for some people not to joke about them. I cannot decide whether or not the late W.G. Sebald would permit himself even the wryest of smiles in response to Woody Allen's parody of Albert Speer's *Inside the Third Reich*.[2] After all, it isn't the Holocaust that 'The Schmeed Memoirs' seeks to extract humour from, rather, Allen is savagely mocking Speer's claim that at the time they were taking place, he personally knew nothing of the murder of the Jews. By transforming Hitler's erstwhile architect – who subsequently became his minister for war production – into a self-deluding barber, Allen performs the essential task of the satirist: to expose the lie of power for what it was, is, and always will be, and to strip away the protective clothing – of idealism, of denial, of retrospective justification – from the perpetrators of genocide.

Ours is an era intoxicated by its capacity to technologically reproduce history, in an instantaneous digitisation of all that has happened. This lays down layer upon layer of decadences. Far from tempering our ability to politicise history, the very existence of this dense stratigraphy seems to spur both individuals and regimes on to still greater tendentiousness. Among modern philosophers Baudrillard understood this development the best, and foresaw the deployment of symbolic events alongside the more conventional weaponry of international conflict.[3]

W.G. Sebald understood it as well: in *The Rings of Saturn* his fictive alter-ego observes the Waterloo Panorama, a 360-degree representation of the battle warped round 'an immense domed rotunda', and muses: 'This then... is the representation of history. It requires a falsification of perspective. We, the survivors, see everything from above, see everything at once, and still we do not know how it was.'[4] To counter this synoptic view – which, again and again throughout his work, Sebald links to dangerous idealisms and utopian fantasies – the writer offered us subjective experience. This was not, however, reportage that relies for its authority on the mere fact of witness; Sebald, as he wrote with reference to the Allied bombing of Hamburg in his essay 'Air War and Literature', mistrusted seeming clarity in the retelling of events that had violently disarranged the senses. Rather, his was a forensic phenomenology that took into account the very lacunae, the repressions and the partial amnesias that are the reality of lived life.[5]

Sebald, perhaps better than anyone, would understand the threshold we are now upon. In 2009 Harry Patch, the final remaining British combatant in the First World War, died, and with the extinguishing of his sentience another stratum of history was sealed shut. In the next two or three decades the same will happen in respect of the Second World War and the Holocaust. Last

November John Demjanjuk was wheeled into a Munich courtroom to stand trial on charges of being an accessory to 27,900 murders in the Sobibor extermination camp, and despite the statement by the Zentralrat der Juden in Deutschland that, 'All NS criminals still living should know that there won't be mercy for them, regardless of their age', it is generally understood that this will be the last Holocaust crimes trial of any significance.

The previous month convicted Holocaust denier Nick Griffin, in his guise as a leader of a legitimate British political party, appeared on BBC1's Question Time, where he was subjected to carefully-orchestrated liberal barracking. And throughout the Christmas period Miroslaw Balka's minatory installation 'How It Is' lowered in the turbine hall of Tate Modern, a steely-black hole in the space-time fabric, beckoning the comfortable London gallery-goers into a psychic identification with those who were forced at gunpoint to entrain for an apocalypse.[6]

And each year on the 27th of January – the anniversary of the Soviet liberation of Auschwitz – we have Holocaust Memorial Day, a national commemoration of the victims of German National Socialism inaugurated by Tony Blair in 2001. W.G. Sebald died in December of that year, but had he lived I doubt he would have made any public comment about this. Nevertheless, while I don't wish to contribute to the world's stock of tendentiousness – of which we already have a superfluity – the message I take from Sebald's works and his scrupulous posture in relation to the remembrance of the Holocaust's victims, is that such events, far from ensuring a 'Legacy of Hope' (the theme of this year's Day), shore up a conception of history, of humanity, and of civilisation that depends on the Holocaust as an exceptional and unprecedented mass murder. It is not just in terms of the Zionist eschatology that the Holocaust is deployed as a symbolic event, but we also require it as a confirmation of our own righteousness in the democratic and industrialised West.

Albert Speer was, of course, the very personification of an industrialisation run amok; a Promethean orgy that saw fire stolen from the Gods and brimstone wrested from the earth. The Nazis, for all the queered atavism of their ideology, were nothing if not modernisers. So, Speer could be significant for Sebald for many reasons – the grotesque giganticism of his designs for the new capital of Hitler's thousand-year Reich would seem the epitome of that bowdlerisation of Burke's 'objects great and terrible' [7] which was the Nazis' vision of art as the servant of social control. In Sebald's *Austerlitz*, the eponymous protagonist, an architectural historian, circles the truth of his origins as he circles the terra incognita of Germany itself. Through his study of such buildings as factories, docks and fortifications hypertrophied by nineteenth century industrialisation, Austerlitz is unconsciously zoning in on the most monstrous disjunction of human scale: the exterminatory assembly-lines of the Holocaust.

Encrypted in Antwerp's Centraal Station Austerlitz finds a programme of social control, and remarks to the novel's narrator:

> The clock is placed some twenty metres above the only baroque element in the entire ensemble, the cruciform stairway which leads from the foyer to the platforms, just where the image of the emperor stood in the Pantheon in a line directly prolonged from the portal; as governor of a new omnipotence it was set even above the royal coat of arms and the motto Eendracht maakt macht.[8]

In English 'Union is strength', but in Flemish it echoes Arbeit macht frei, just as Austerlitz is a near homophone for Auschwitz.

Then, there is Speer's awkward status as not only the preeminent German denier of Holocaust knowledge, but also its foremost passive resister, who, charged with Hitler's scorched earth policy, saved as much of its industrial infrastructure as he could. Just as Speer refused the evidence of his own senses when he visited the slave labourers at the notorious Mittelbau-Dora missile factory, so we can imagine that Sebald's own father refused – at least in retrospect – to acknowledge the reality of what he witnessed as a career soldier in the Wermacht.

Sebald said of his own parents that they were typical of German petit-bourgeois who 'went into the war not just blindly, but with a degree of enthusiasm… they all felt they were going to be lords of the world'. Sebald's father was in the Polish campaign, and in the family photo album there were pictures that initially had a 'boy scout atmosphere', but:

Then the order came, and they moved in. And now the photographs are of Polish villages instead, razed to the ground, with only the chimneys left standing. These photos seemed quite normal to me as a child... I look at them now, and I think, 'Good Lord, what is all this?' [9]

It's easy to see this as Sebald's paradigmatic experience of the power of photography to both document and dissemble historical reality – power he himself would make great use of. In *Vertigo* Sebald's alter-ego says of an album that his father bought his mother in 1939 as a present for the first Kriegsweihnacht – or Nazi-sanctioned 'War Christmas':

Some of these photographs show gypsies who had been rounded up and put in detention. They are looking out, smiling from behind the barbed wire, somewhere in a far corner of the Slovakia where my father and his vehicle repairs unit had been stationed for several weeks before the outbreak of war.[10]

And there, below the text, is the photograph in question, which was, Sebald said in an interview: 'an indication that these things were accepted as part of the operation right from the beginning'.[11]

Named 'Winfried' from a Nazi list of approved names, and 'Georg' after his father, Sebald preferred to be known as Max. Born in the Bavarian Alps in May 1944, as the Reich was collapsing beneath the allied onslaught, his own literary achievement stands in almost diametric opposition to that of Speer. While Speer occupied himself exclusively with variations on the theme of what the psychoanalytic thinker Alexander Mitscherlich termed his Lebenslüge, or 'Great Lie',[12/163] Sebald devoted his energies to exposing all the smaller lies of his parents' generation. He remained steadfast in his excoriation: when asked in the course of an interview with the *Jewish Quarterly* after the publication of *The Emigrants* whether he could talk to his parents about the so-called 'Hitler time', Sebald replied:

Not really. Though my father is still alive, at eighty-five... it's the ones who have a conscience who die early, it grinds you down. The fascist supporters live forever. Or the passive resisters. That's what they all are now in their own minds. I always try to explain to my parents that there is no difference between passive resistance and passive collaboration – it's the same thing. But they cannot understand that.[13]

There is, as yet, no direct access to Georg Sebald's war record, but sifting through the clues in Sebald's texts and cross-referencing these with his statements in interviews, it seems likely to me that his father ended up serving with the 1st Gerbirgsjäger – or 'mountain huntsmen' – who were indeed stationed in Slovakia before the invasion of Poland, and whose war record includes a sorry tapestry of war crimes, including the rounding up and shooting of Jews in Lvov. Sebald, inevitably, was not close to his father, who had been taken prisoner by the Americans in 1945 and only returned home when the writer was three. But while it's almost a cliché to say of a male writer's books that they are acts of parricide, Sebald's great achievement lay in not succumbing to Oedipal rage so as to forestall tragic sadness.

In the years since Max Sebald's untimely death his status – already high – has increased. In 2007 Horace Engdahl, former secretary of the Swedish Academy, cited Sebald as one of the writers who would have been a worthy Nobel laureate.[14] I don't take issue with this; however I am interested in saving Sebald from the ossification of this kind of critical regard which is the preserve of arts functionaries and their selective lists. As I've had cause to remark before: it's pets that win prizes, and I don't believe that Sebald was anyone's pet. Rather, let us resurrect him as a disciple of the writer and Holocaust survivor Jean Améry, of whom Sebald wrote, '[His] existentialist philosophical position... makes no concessions to history but exemplifies the necessity of continuing to protest, a dimension so strikingly lacking from German post-war literature.'[15]

Sebald is rightly seen as the non-Jewish German writer who through his works did most to mourn the murder of the Jews. He said that he felt no guilt himself – and indeed why should he? he wasn't responsible – but that there was an irremediable 'sense of shame'. Subjected at school, as all Germans of his generation were, to a film of the concentration camps without explanation or contextualisation, Sebald was jolted out of what had been an isolated bucolic childhood; it impinged on him from then on that:

> While I was sitting in my pushchair and being wheeled through the flowering meadows by my mother, the Jews of Corfu were being deported on a four-week trek to Poland. It is the simultaneity of a blissful childhood and those horrific events that now strikes me as incomprehensible. I know now that these things cast a very long shadow over my life.[16]

The shadow lengthened through his university career where, in Freiburg, Sebald found himself being taught German literature by academics he later described as 'dissembling old fascists'.[17] Only the returned exile Theodor Adorno offered any insight, and no doubt his remarks on the possibility of a post-Holocaust literature must have been something the young Sebald took to heart: 'To write poetry after Auschwitz,' Adorno wrote, 'is barbaric.'[18] A statement he later amplified thus: 'The so-called artistic rendering of the naked physical pain of those who were beaten down with rifle butts contains, however distantly, the possibility that pleasure can be squeezed from it.'[19]

Such 'action writing', and any possible voyeurism, were modes that subsequently Sebald carefully avoided – just as he himself never visited a concentration camp. This was a pilgrimage that Sebald believed was 'not the answer',[20] especially since such sites had become only way-stations on the profaning tourist trail. I wish I had the time here to plot carefully the journey that Sebald did undertake, from Freiburg to Francophone Switzerland where he completed his degree, and from there, in 1966, to Manchester where he became a teaching assistant and finished his masters. He returned briefly to Switzerland for an unsatisfactory Wittgensteinian experiment in school teaching, before going back to Manchester and then on to the University of East Anglia, where, apart from a spell in Munich at the Goethe Institute in 1975-6, he remained for the rest of his life.

I wish I also had the time to exhaustively map his intellectual and literary development, but for the purposes of my argument here a couple of significant episodes will have to suffice. First, there was Sebald's exposure to the Auschwitz-

Birkenau trials of 1963-5 in Munich, which he followed assiduously in the newspapers. Sebald said of the trials: 'it was the first public acknowledgement that there was such a thing as an unresolved German past'. And further that, 'I realised there were things of much greater urgency than the writings of the German Romantics'.[21] Sebald was struck both by the utter familiarity of the defendants – 'the kinds of people I'd known as neighbours' – but still more by how the Jewish witnesses, initially strange and foreign, were in the course of the proceedings revealed to have been residents of Nuremberg and Stuttgart. For Sebald, awakening to the realisation that he had been living among tacit accomplices to the elimination of these people's relatives, made him feel himself to be a tacit accomplice as well, and so he 'had to know what had happened in detail, and try to understand why it should have been so'.[22]

We will return to that 'why', which I believe to be crucial, because with a less nakedly philosophic writer it would undoubtedly have been replaced by the 'how' of historicist instrumentality. But in the meantime let us consider Sebald's move to Britain, and in particular to Manchester, which in 1966 – as today – had a thriving Jewish community. In postwar Germany it was, of course, only too possible never to encounter a Jew, but now Sebald had a German Jewish landlord whose own parents had been deported to Riga where they were murdered. This man subsequently became one of the models for Max Ferber, the painter in Sebald's *The Emigrants,* and the encounter hammered home the template for his subsequent modus operandi: 'To my mind,' Sebald later said, 'there is an acute difference between historiography and history as experienced history.'[23]

The experience of real, live, Jews was definitely important – and possibly equally significant was that these were English Jews; after all, if, as the old Jewish saying has it, the Jews are like everyone else but more so, then it can be inferred that English Jews are like the English – but more so. The uncanny portrayal of Dr Henry Selwyn in *The Emigrants* is a function of his almost perfect assimilation to English diffidence, and since Sebald based him on a real-life model who the writer did not even realise was of Polish-Jewish extraction until told so, he stands as a sign pointing towards that earlier age when German Jews, with names such as Hamburger and Berlin – evidence, Sebald once remarked, of just how tragically close their identification with the Fatherland was – were quite as well camouflaged.

This is not to say that Sebald's Jews are anything but individuals. For a counterexample to his own meticulousness you can look no further than Bernard Schlink's *The Reader*,[24] a novel widely feted for its moving portrayal of the impact of the Holocaust – but on whom, exactly? Schlink's novel may present a schema of evolving Holocaust consciousness in the successor generation of Germans, but its effects depend on exactly the kind of 'action writing' that Sebald rejected. In Schlink's case this 'action' consists in the frisson of the protagonist's underage sex with a beautiful concentration camp guard. No wonder Schlink's novel became that tiresome cliché 'a major motion picture', complete with a Titanic English actress indulging in artistic nudity. It is perhaps to Schlink's credit that he doesn't try and pretend sufficient familiarity with the sole Jewish character in the novel to actually provide her with a name; but, as some critics have done, to credit this as a sensitive allegory – one individual in lieu of the exterminated six million – seems special pleading to me.

Of course, in his writings and interviews Sebald never pretended that his artistic development was entirely sui generis; it's more that the lamentable insularity of the English-speaking world – if we can speak of something so mondial as an island – has made us generally impervious to foreign cultural influences that depend vitally on language. This cannot have been far from Sebald's own mind, not only when he rigorously collaborated on the translations of his own prose fictions from German into English, but also in his work as a pedagogue and as the founder, in 1989, of the British Centre for Literary Translation at the University of East Anglia.

Be that as it may, the influence of Alexander Kluge – to name but one exemplar of the documentary literature of postwar Germany – on Sebald's methodology and concerns is difficult to assess for a non-German speaker, since none of Kluge's key texts are available in translation. We can identify, to some extent, Sebald's affinities with Jean Améry, or with Alfred Döblin, the subject of his own doctoral thesis, but the point needs to be stressed that these are Jewish German writers, the former a Holocaust survivor, the latter a Modernist whose sensibility was shaped during Weimar. What we cannot do is to place Sebald within the German literary context where he might be said to belong.

In cosmology there is what's known as 'the strong anthropic argument', which extrapolates from the coincidence of the physical laws of the universe and our ability to observe those laws, to the proposition that this is no coincidence but a necessity: the universe has evolved precisely to produce beings of our kind, QED, God. I suspect in our view of W.G. Sebald as the preeminent – or at least most widely and obvious revered – German language writer in the English speaking world, we are falling victim to a strong anthropic argument, when a weaker one will suffice.

Undoubtedly, it was precisely Sebald's own exile from Germany and his exposure to living Jewish communities that made it possible for him to transform the inchoate mistrust of his 'passive collaborator' background into an active literature of atonement. I suspect there is a degree of wishful thinking in the critiques of postwar German literature published in English, and the title of the most comprehensive of these – Ernestine Schlant's worthy if over-determined *The Language of Silence* [25] – says it all. The literature of Holocaust survivors can tell us how it was, but it can do little to explain why it was, for that we have impotently required a fully self-actualised literature of the perpetrators; in other words: an impossibility. Hannah Arendt's much quoted subtitle to her study of the Eichmann trial, *the banality of evil*, has become a shibboleth to be lisped in the nightmarish face of the Holocaust. In fact, Arendt avoided the term in the text, while stressing in her private letters from Jerusalem during the trial that, after ploughing through the 3,000-page transcript of Eichmann's interrogation by the Israeli police, what impressed her most was his 'brainlessness'.[26]

We cannot interrogate the brainless for their or our own self-actualisation, we cannot look to those who have capitulated to a regime which made evil a form of civil norm for a moral re-evaluation. Instead, we have their sons and daughters, and we have Sebald; whose elegant, elegiac and haunting prose narratives reinstate the prelapsarian German-speaking world. His careful use of documentary sources places before the contemporary reader the actualité of a culture in which Jews were an integral part, while his style is at once discursive – looping in historic anecdote and literary reference – and incisive: cutting away at the surface of reality to expose the mysterious interconnections of things-in-themselves. To read Sebald is to be confronted with European history not as an ideologically determined diachronic – as proposed by Hegelians and Spenglerians alike – nor as a synchronic phenomenon to be subjected to Baudrillard's postmodern analysis. Rather, for Sebald, history is a palimpsest – and the reification implied is significant – the meaning of which can only be divined by rubbing away a little bit here, adding on some over there, and then – most importantly – stepping back to allow for a synoptic view that remains inherently suspect.

I think it's this beguiling overview – which Sebald calls our attention to again and again in his writings by describing the works of Dutch landscape painters and English watercolourists – that explains in part our willingness to ascribe to him some specifically moral ascendancy, and, by implication, a historiography he explicitly denies. For the English-speaking world – and the English in particular – Sebald is the longed for 'Good German'; he's everything Speer wanted to become but never could. Sebald has recognised the taint and moved to erase it by a systematic bearing of witness. But if he had remained behind in Germany, might he not have succumbed to the same pressures as many of his generation, and been carried along on the tide of Marxian posturing to a fallacious equivalence of the Federal Republic with the Third Reich? It's hard to imagine Sebald subsuming the emotional reality of the Holocaust to an intellectual abstraction, just as it's difficult to see him falling for the victimology of many German writers of the successor generation, who, in their torturous investigations of Oedipal hatred, revealed only that it was all about them.

But then, recall that Sebald was no great believer in freewill. 'This notion,' he said, 'of the autonomous individual who is in charge of his or her fate is one that I couldn't really subscribe to.'[27] So presumably nor could he have subscribed to any view of his literary work as originating from a desire to do the right thing – that was then done. Indeed he never did: he disavowed any particular philo-Semitism, explaining his resurrection of German Jewry as a form of social history as much as anything else – which does indeed make Sebald sound more English than the English. But the urge to project holy motives on to writers in this godless age is quite as strong as our desire to damn them to a hell no one believes in either.

In England, Sebald's onetime presence among us – even if we would never be so crass as to think this, let alone articulate it – is registered as further confirmation that we won, and won because of our righteousness, our liberality, our inclusiveness and our tolerance. Where else would the Good German have sprouted so readily, if not from our brown and nutritious soil? If he had remained at home might he not have become – at the very least – a German version of Thomas Bernhard, a refusenik, an internal exile, his solipsism not modulated by melancholy but intensified until it became a cachinnating cynicism? Instead, the writing is anecdotal in feel, and furnished with plenty of English quotidiana – teasmaids and coal fires, battered cod and dotty prep school masters, branch line rail journeys and model-making enthusiasts; enough, at any rate, to submerge any disquieting philosophising.

I might be doing the mittel-English readership of Sebald – if indeed such people exist at all – a disservice, were it not that I'm prepared to take the rap myself: I find Sebald's path into the charnel house of the twentieth century quite reassuring – especially when it takes the form of a hearty English walk. To read exclusively German postwar German literature is to find myself in the position of the unnamed narrator of Walter Abish's *How German is It?*, who, on returning to his hometown after the war, becomes transfixed by the way Germanness inheres in everything he sets his eyes on – even the rivets that secure the map of the town to the station wall.[28]

In too-German Germany Sebald is, of course, not quite German enough. In recent years there has been some upgrading of his reputation, but Sebald would've needed to be alive in order to have benefited from Gunter Grass's own downgrading following the revelation of his SS membership. As for Martin Walser, paradoxically it is his insistence that Germans have done enough atoning which – or so German friends of mine assure me – people find 'boring'.

Sebald did enter the lists of the great controversies surrounding the history of the Hitler-time when in 1997 he delivered his series of Zurich lectures, posthumously published in English in an edited form, under the title *On the Natural History of Destruction*. When these writings appeared in Germany, Sebald's contention that the wholesale destruction of the German cities by Allied bombing, resulting in 600,000 civilian deaths and five million homeless, was singularly under-represented in postwar German literature became a stick in the hands of both right and left, intent on beating on each other. Sebald's reputation predictably suffered collateral damage. I suspect Sebald was not so much ingenuous as out of touch with contemporary opinion: to him the continuing and plangent shame Germans should feel for the murder of the Jews remained a given; it did not need to be restated in a thesis concerning a different mass killing. Besides, he did state explicitly in the text that it ill-behoved Germans to castigate the wartime allies – whatever their motivation – for prosecuting the war in this fashion.

You don't have to be an exile to be perceived as a Nestbeschmutzer (one who dirties his own nest) in the German-speaking world – but it helps; while exactly those Bakelite touches English critics find reassuring – even as they shade-in the utter blackness – German ones are dismissive of. Reviewing *Austerlitz* for *Die Zeit*, Iris Radisch described its lapidary style as 'Holocaust and staghorn buttons' while averring that, 'Something's wrong here... Is it really possible to use the same model of archives to describe the search for your deported parents as the search for shells... in a school friend's house? ... Is it persuasive to plaster the journey back to the places of expulsion, death and destruction with antique curiosities?'

Then again, given that if you hale a cab outside Frankfurt's rail station its driver is very likely to be writing a doctoral thesis on the Frankfurt School, Sebald's metaphysical bent – worrying to English empiricists – is viewed straightforwardly by this compatriot: 'Sebald is the same as those philosophers, of whom Kierkegaard said, all that they write about reality is just as confusing as reading a sign at a flea market stall that says "Washing done here". You come back with your things, hoping to have them washed, but instead you stand there like an idiot because the sign is merely there to be sold.'[29]

None of which is to suggest that you cannot also find plenty of praise for Sebald's works among German critics, it's just that what's missing is the peculiar reverence that attaches to writings that – so long as they aren't read too closely – seem to confirm us English in some of our most comforting prejudices. Context, as Sebald himself knew, remains only too important, and before I reach the kernel of my thesis concerning W.G. Sebald and the Holocaust I think it only fair to limn in my own. How English is that?

I began with a quote from a Woody Allen parody that I first read in his anthology *Getting Even* soon after its publication in 1971. I found 'The Schmeed Memoirs' uproariously funny, although aged eleven I had no idea who Albert Speer was. I did however have an awareness of the Holocaust – not least because my mother had told me for as long as I could remember that the Polish woman who lived alone in the detached house at the end of our block was a camp survivor. And moreover, that the reason why this woman's privet hedge was so spectacularly neglected was that she feared the return of the Nazis, and believed that they would – like the Angel of Death – pass by if they thought no one lived there.

I've no idea if any of this was true – my mother had a flair for dramatics – but it seemed credible, given that whenever I saw the Polish woman, her tightly-belted grey gabardine raincoat and short, lank, dyed-black hair gave her a curiously anachronistic appearance, as if she were a black-and-white photograph pasted on to the verdant Ektachrome of the Hampstead Garden Suburb. I also knew about the 'passive collaborators' with the Holocaust from an early age – because my mother regularly accused my father of having been one.

In retrospect, and in the full light of the knowledge I now possess concerning the political consciousness of upper-middle-class English ex-public schoolboys in the late 1930s, this notion of my mother's is not just preposterous – but hateful. My father was twenty in 1939 when his call-up papers arrived. He had just gone up for his first term at Oxford, and had for some time been a member of Dick Sheppard's Peace Pledge Union. He told me before he died that during the week after his call-up arrived he was wracked by doubts about what he should do, but in the end he decided to register as a conscientious objector. Intermittently, but with greater intensity as the years had passed, he had regretted this.

For my mother, an American Jew of Russian extraction, ignorance was no defence when it came to the Nazis' genocidal intentions towards Jewry, and therefore my father was exactly like those Germans who claimed to have been unaware of the mass murders even after they had occurred. While accepting that she, growing up in the New York borough of Queens in the 1930s, may well have been aware of the Nazis' persecutory zeal, because – as she told me – of letters our relatives in Europe were forced to send requesting money that was then stolen from them, I realised when I came to study the Holocaust in detail that neither she – nor indeed anyone, save possibly Hitler himself – could have known in 1939 that the Nazis' Final Solution would necessarily be an exterminatory one. This being noted, my father's further claim that he knew nothing at all of the Holocaust until Richard Dimbleby's famous broadcasts from Belsen in 1945 does suggest a certain willed ignorance on his part, which, if not exactly Speer-like, was far from uncommon among the British.

I don't wish to make too much of this; looked at one way there is something merely sad about such implausible culpability becoming domestic mud slung in a miserable marriage, but looked at differently it taught me early on to mistrust arguments founded on spuriously synoptic historical schemas, and to have my doubts when it came to the idea that the German's murdering of the Jews possessed any absolute exceptionality. Not that my mother – wilfully deracinated as she was – cleaved to any Jewish eschatology, Zionist or otherwise. Nor can I say that she ever articulated the conventional formulation of Holocaust remembrance: these things must never be forgotten, lest they occur again.

In *The Rings of Saturn*, W.G. Sebald cryptically alludes to Jorge Luis Borges's story 'Tlön Uqbar Orbis Tertius', which, in a typically Borgesian fashion, plays with the idea of an idealist world created by eighteenth century encyclopaedists to bedevil their empiricist heirs. The passage Sebald had in mind was this:

> Things became duplicated in Tlön; they also tend to become effaced and lose their details when they are forgotten. A classic example is the doorway which survived so long it was visited by a beggar and disappeared at his death. At times some birds, a horse, have saved the ruins of an amphitheatre.[30]

In the preamble to this same strange tale Borges's narrator recalls a dinner with a friend at which

> ...we became lengthily engaged in a vast polemic concerning the composition of a novel in the first person, whose narrator would omit or disfigure the facts and indulge in various contradictions which would permit a few readers – very few readers – to perceive an atrocious or banal reality.[31]

This is of course W.G. Sebald's own fictive methodology, and I believe only a very few readers have grasped the atrocious and banal reality that he wishes us to perceive, despite the myriad clues that are scattered throughout his texts.

Consider this, from *Austerlitz*, where the eponymous survivor of the Kindertransport remarks,

> It does not seem to me... that we understand the laws governing the return of the past, but I feel more and more as if time did not exist at all, only various spaces interlocking according to the rules of a higher form of stereometry, between which the living and the dead can move back and forth as they like, and the longer I think about it the more it seems to me that we who are still alive are unreal in the eyes of the dead. [32]

Again and again Sebald makes statements of a transcendental idealism, again and again he points to coincidence and déjà vu as evidence of the unheimlich quality of subjectivity. This is Sebald's alter-ego in *The Rings of Saturn:*

> ...my rational mind is... unable to lay the ghosts of repetition that haunt me with ever greater frequency. Scarcely am I in company but it seems as if I had already heard the same opinions expressed by the same people somewhere or other, in the same way, with the same words, turns of phrase and gestures. [33]

If instead of conventional linear narratives Sebald's prose fictions are word-filigrees spun out of such atemporal coincidences, then they are also haunted by the congruence of the things-in-themselves that constitute the material world: In *The Emigrants* Max Ferber returns to smoky industrial Manchester, understanding intuitively that while he may have escaped the Holocaust, it remains his destiny to 'serve under the chimney'.[34]

The echo of the Buna at Auschwitz is certainly intentional, and just as willed by Sebald are the references throughout his books to Theresienstadt, the 'model' concentration camp established by Reinhardt Heydrich in the Bohemian hinterland. I speak not just of the extended passages concerning the camp in *Austerlitz*, but of tens and scores of other references to it – far more than to any of the other, more notorious nodes of the Holocaust. I believe that in Theresienstadt, where tens of thousands of 'privileged' Jews were crammed into an eighteenth century fortified town a kilometre square, Sebald saw the very synecdoche of the Holocaust.

With its theatre company and orchestra, its workshops and its newspaper, Theresienstadt was given a grotesque make-over by the Germans so that it could serve as a Potemkin village for a Red Cross inspection in 1944 designed to allay international suspicions. At the same time a film was made depicting the idyllic existence of those who shortly after the shooting stopped were transported to the gas chambers of Auschwitz, or else forced east on the death marches that claimed 1.5 million more Jewish lives in the Nazis' Gotterdammerung.

Theresienstadt is for Sebald only an extreme and specialised form of a Holocaust he sees being perpetrated everywhere and at all times as civilization marches on. If there is any exceptional character to the German Holocaust it is only that it is German, just as Belgian holocausts are Belgian, Rwandan ones Rwandan, and Croatian ones – albeit under German tutelage – are Croatian. Describing Joseph Conrad's arrival in Brussels to take up the commission which would gain him the material for *Heart of Darkness*,[35] Sebald wrote:

> [Conrad] now saw the capital of the Kingdom of Belgium, with its ever more bombastic buildings, as a sepulchral monument erected over a hecatomb of black bodies, and all the passers-by in the streets seemed to him to bear that dark Congolese secret within them.[36]

While historians such as Daniel Jonah Goldhagen might wish to arrogate a unique exterminatory impulse to the Germans,[37] Sebald resists this facile view at every juncture. In his doctoral thesis on Alfred Döblin, Sebald was inclined to see aspects of *Berlin Alexanderplatz* as a shadow cast forwards, a kind of reverse memory. Commenting on Döblin's description of an abattoir Sebald avers that 'Far more horrifying than the chaotic destruction of the Apocalypse is the well-ordered destruction contrived by man himself.'[38]

Implicit in Sebald's work is the idea that human mass-murder is only a suicidal form of the holocaust we are perpetrating on the natural world. It is there in *The Rings of Saturn* where the description of the destruction of the European fisheries is juxtaposed with a double-page photograph of the naked bodies of the Nazis' victim lying among trees.[39] It is there in *The Emigrants* where Manchester is described as a 'necropolis or mausoleum';[40] in *Vertigo* also when the vehicles crawling along the gleaming black roads out of Innsbruck are imagined as 'the last of an amphibian species close to extinction'.[41] Encrypted in almost every line of *After Nature* we find the same message:

> Cities phosphorescent / on the riverbank, industry's / glowing piles waiting / beneath the smoke trails / like ocean giants for the siren's / blare, the twitching lights / of rail- and motorways, the murmur / of the millionfold proliferating molluscs, / woodlice and leeches, the cold putrefaction [42]

In conclusion then, W.G. Sebald had no need of a Holocaust Remembrance Day – and I believe that if we read him rightly nor have we English. In Germany a Memorial Day for the Victims of National Socialism is indeed an appropriate response – if not an atonement – for crimes committed, but here Tony Blair might have done better to inaugurate a Refusal to Grant Refugee Jews Asylum Memorial Day, or an Incendiary Bombing of German Cities Memorial Day, or even – casting the shadow forward – an Iraqi Civilians Killed Due to Pusillanimous Atlanticist Foreign Policy Memorial Day, for these are deaths that more properly belong at our door.

For Sebald and for those of us who hearken to his metaphysic, there is no need to remember because the Nazis' Holocaust is still happening in an interlocking space, while right beside us are the poisoned seas, the glowing piles and the cold putrefaction of an environmental one. 'More and more,' the narrator of *The Emigrants* tells us concerning Dr Selwyn, 'he sensed that Nature itself was groaning and collapsing beneath the burden we placed upon it.' [43] And as Gerhard Richter's fusion of slow oils and photographic quicksilver so perfectly expresses, upon that denuded foreground, Onkel Rudi is always posing for the camera, smiling, in front of the slave labourers' hecatomb.[44]

---

[1] Woody Allen 'The Schmeed Memoirs' *Getting Even* (London, Picador: 1993), pp. 21-26; p.22

[2] Albert Speer *Inside the Third Reich* (New York, Macmillan: 1970).

[3] See e.g. Jean Baudrillard *The Gulf War Did Not Take Place* (Bloomington, Indiana UP: 1995).

[4] *The Rings of Saturn*, pp.124-5.

[5] *On the Natural History of Destruction*, pp.1-106.

[6] Miroslaw Balka 'How It Is' (2009) [sculptural installation] London: Tate Modern.

[7] Edmund Burke *Philosophical Enquiry into the Origin of our Ideas of the Sublime and the Beautiful: with an introductory discourse concerning taste, and several other additions* (London: G & W.B. Whittaker, 1821), p.151. First published 1757

[8] *Austerlitz*, p.13.

[9] Sebald in conversation with Carole Angier in 'Who is W.G. Sebald?' *The Emergence of Memory: Conversations with W.G. Sebald*. Ed. Lynne Sharon Schwartz (New York, Seven Stories: 2007), pp.63-75; pp.66-7.

[10] *Vertigo*, p.184.

[11] Sebald in conversation with Christoper Bigsby 'In Conversation with W.G. Sebald' *Writers in Conversation with Christopher Bigsby*, Vol. 2. (Norwich, Arthur Miller Centre for American Studies: 2001), pp.139-165; p.145.

[12] Gitta Sereny *Albert Speer: His Battle with Truth* (London, Picador: 1996), p. 704. See also pp.388-407.

[13] 'Who is W.G. Sebald?', p.67.

[14] Horace Engdahl, Interview, *Vi* (2007)

[15] *On the Natural History of Destruction*, p.160.

[16] 'In Conversation with W.G. Sebald', p.144.

[17] Sebald in conversation with Toby Green 'The Questionable Business of Writing' [online] available from http://www.amazon.co.uk/gp/feature.html?ie=UTF8&docId=21586 accessed 12 September 2013.

[18] Theodor Adorno 'Cultural Criticism and Society' *Prisms* (Cambridge MA, MIT: 1981), pp.17-35; p.34.

[19] Theodor Adorno 'Commitment' *Can One Live after Auschwitz?*: A Philosophical Reader (California, Stanford UP:2003), pp.240-258; p. 252.

[20] 'In Conversation with W.G. Sebald', p.146.

[21] *Ibid*, p.147.

22 Sebald in conversation with Maya Jaggi 'Recovered Memories' *The Guardian* (22 September 2001).
23 Sebald in conversation with Christopher Bigsby in 'W.G. Sebald: an act of restitution' *Remembering and Imagining the Holocaust: the chain of memory* (Cambridge, CUP: 2006), pp.25-114; p.35.
24 Bernard Schlink *The Reader*, trans Carol Brown Janeway, (London, Phoenix House: 1997).
25 Ernestine Schlant *The Language of Silence* (New York, Routledge: 1999).
26 Amos Elon 'The Excommunication of Hannah Arendt' in Hannah Arendt *Eichmann in Jerusalem: a report on the Banality of Evil* (New York, Penguin: 2006), pp.vii-xxiii; p.xiii. Eichmann in Jerusalem first published 1963.
27 Sebald in conversation with Joseph Cuomo 'A Conversation with W.G. Sebald' *The Emergence of Memory*, pp.93-117; p.117.
28 Walter Abish *How German Is It: Wie Deutsch Ist Est* (New York, New Directions: 1979).
29 Iris Radisch 'Der Waschbär der falschen Welt: W. G. Sebald sammelt Andenken und rettet die Vergangenheit vorm Vergehen' *Die Zeit* (5 April 2001).
30 Jorge Luis Borges 'Tlön, Uqbar, Orbis Tertius' *Labyrinths* (New York, New Directions: 1964), pp.27-44; p.39.
31 *Ibid*, p.27.
32 *Austerlitz*, p.261.
33 *The Rings of Saturn*, p.187.
34 *The Emigrants*, p.192.
35 Joseph Conrad *Heart of Darkness* (London, Penguin:1995) First published in 1902.
36 *The Rings of Saturn*, p.122.
37 Daniel Jonah Goldhagen *Hitler's Willing Executioners: Ordinary Germans and the Holocaust* (New York, Alfred A Knopf: 1996).
38 *The Revival of Myth: A Study of Döblin's Novels*, Ph.D thesis (University of East Anglia: 1973), p.68.
39 *The Rings of Saturn*, pp.55-61.
40 *The Emigrants*, p.151.
41 *Vertigo*, p.172.
42 *After Nature*, p.109-10.
43 *The Emigrants*, p.7.
44 Gerhard Richter 'Onkel Rudi' (1965) [oil on canvas] Lidice, Czech Republic: Lidice Gallery.

AFTER SEBALD

Richard Long

✻

LIFEDEATH

Clive Scott

*

W.G. Sebald: Enumeration, Photography and the Hermeneutics of History

Sir Thomas Browne's thoughts on error, including the making of knowledge by oblivion, the clash between the unruliness of ongoing experience and the guiding light of acquired precepts, and the prevailing existential acknowledgement 'that we find no open tract or constant manuduction in this labyrinth, but are ofttimes fain to wander in the America and untravelled parts of truth',[1] cannot but be powerfully suggestive for a reading of W.G. Sebald. And what Sebald says of Browne's style – its funereal ceremoniousness, its double focus (long range/close up) and polarised moods ('gravitation' [nicht immer, von der Erde abzuheben]/levitation)[2] – clearly resonates in his own hypotactic habits.[3] Double focus and polarised moods are central to a consideration of the mechanism of enumeration in Sebald's writing.

The enumerative principle makes itself manifest in many different Sebaldian institutions and activities: the artist's studio, the graveyard, the collection, the repository, the library, the museum, the catalogue, the treasury, the inventory, the dictionary, the encyclopaedia, the emporium, the pawnshop, the second-hand shop (where Sebald is in the habit of picking up old photos),[4] the antiques shop, the country house, the attic and the photo-album. There are obvious connections between enumeration and the archive, so fruitfully explored by Jonathan Long,[5] but my approach to enumeration is not primarily concerned with the archival mentality, with classification and preservation, nor with the archive as organ of discipline and control (the Foucauldian framework); enumeration here is treated as an existential pivot, a perceptual crux which generates a dialectic between the paratactic (close-up) and the hypotactic (the long view), between a jamming mechanism and the flow of history.

Enumeration frequently deals with objects which have fallen into disuse, which have lost their dynamic and acquired an inertial state; this is where their power of 'gravitation' lies. They are objects without syntactic intricacy, impediments to hypotaxis, which is the record of a mental activity, of processes of 'plotting', and of the extraction or projection of meaning, by relational arrangement. Enumeration pushes aside the ratiocinative mind, and human agency more generally; and in the place of the syntax of teleology and controlled temporalities and interpretative processing, enumeration, the sequence of photos, installs a paratactic montage of indefinite limits, a problematic temporality, a spirit of contingency which poses searching questions about continuity, function, epistemology: enumeration does not tell us what type of knowledge we have of things, nor what makes things meaningful for us. The energy of accumulation, of integration into a living structure, into a network of significant connections and acquisitional situations, gradually, it seems, degenerates into the need to sell off, to disperse, or merely to neglect. Somerleyton Hall is witness to such a degenerative process:

> As I strolled through Somerleyton Hall that August afternoon, amidst a throng of visitors who occasionally lingered here or there, I was variously reminded of a pawnbroker's or an auction hall. And yet it was the sheer number of things, possessions accumulated by generations and now waiting, as it were, for the day when they would be sold off, that won me over to what was, ultimately, a collection of oddities. [6]

One of the things that is left behind at Somerleyton is a solitary, caged Chinese quail, or, one might say, the photo of a Chinese quail. For photographs seem, more generally, like relics, a jetsam unlikely to find its beachcomber, and as direct expressions of the enumerative, they are evidences and instruments of a larger entropic condition in which, as energy declines, so randomness and the likelihood of oblivion increase.

The overall experience of Somerleyton is prefigured in the exploration of the attic of the Alpenrose in 'Il ritorno in patria' [7], where the accumulated objects have undergone a physical deterioration, 'Zeichen einer langsamen Auflösung in die auf dem Dachboden herrschende völlige Stille' [8] [tokens of the slow disintegration of all material forms in the complete silence of this attic [9]]. It is as if the narrator will not be able to plumb their past ('die mögliche Herkunft und Geschichte dieser Dinge' [10] [the possible provenance and history of these items [11]]) before their future has reduced them to dust or otherwise put them beyond salvage. And yet, and yet. In the word 'Auflösung' might be heard a different note: not just disintegration and dissolution, but solution and resolution, a way forward out of oblivion. For the narrator also experiences the brimming resurgence of objects: 'quoll alles nur Erdenkliche an Gebrauchsgegenständen und Kleidungsstücken' [12] [all conceivable kinds of utensils and garments were bursting forth [13]]. This phrase throws us back to the phrase Sebald has used two pages earlier about the atlas, about barely discovered territories and the only partly decipherable legends which make them seem 'alles an Geheimnisse nur Ausdenkbare zu enthalten' [14] [to hold in them all conceivable mysteries [15]]. The objects in the attic are as if in movement, evolving, playing 'statues' with us, reinventing coordinates, drawn by the magnet of their elective affinities. Here, gravitation moves into the levitation of the 'all conceivable'. And, indeed, our previous quotation about Somerleyton is not unmitigatedly negative: the narrator begins to suggest a transformation whereby possessions, ripe for the pawnbroker's or auction room, become 'a collection of oddities'. Enumeration contains within itself the principle of catalysm, whereby, thanks to human agency, things apparently marooned from each other can enter into fruitful contacts. Enumeration as the fateful undoing of the syntactically articulated is countered by enumeration as a putting at our creative disposal; the difficult obligations of the reconstruction of history are constantly diverted into the free-wheeling challenge of making possible futures.

Thus, while Deane Blackler is right to speak of the contrary impulses of the paratactic and the hypotactic (discontinuity v. continuity), and to equate photographs with the paratactic,[16] it is perhaps more just to speak of their evolutionary relationship: as hypotaxis dies into parataxis, so parataxis is resurrected into hypotaxis. Enumeration is then terminal and liminal, the two faces of 'Auflösung', the point at which inert juxtaposition becomes challenging montage. Montage is what Bailly calls a 'champ herméneutique entièrement nouveau' [an entirely new hermeneutic field].[17] Every image/object, even the most humble snapshot, has other images/objects in its field of activity or energy. In this weave of connections, chronology is set aside, objects and photos recover a mobility which runs counter to the stasis of their morbidity and relaunches history in the form of histories.[18] In other words, every image/object is writing two histories: the one of its indexicality[19] and the other of its intertextuality, the one of its overtness, the other of its latency.

How then does it come about that enumeration institutes a new hermeneutics of history? When we think of enumeration in relation to double focus, it may be natural to reckon that the long view, the totalising view, is supplied by *exhaustive* and articulated enumeration, by the ability to list *all* components, to circumscribe and make sense; and that, correspondingly the microscopic view relates to *non-exhaustive* or inexhaustible enumeration: we see things in front of us, one by one, without knowing how many or in what configuration, or when the list will stop, or what has been left out. But in actual fact, all enumeration is non-exhaustive. If we possess five photos of a particular event, we know we have not seen all there is to see, and we have no idea how many other photos have yet to surface. Reality is itself an inexhaustible repository. The narrator tells Lukas: 'The more images I gathered from the past, I said, the more unlikely it seemed to me that the past had happened in this or that way, for nothing about it could be called normal: most of it was absurd, and if not absurd, then appalling.'[20] Enumeration is the process whereby we register our sense of being outnumbered, overwhelmed by a constant movement of proliferation. And the animism with which Sebald invests inanimate objects expresses itself in the ability of objects themselves to bear witness, to assimilate what they have seen. Photographs do not record memories, they remember us, and go on remembering, in their lives as objects. How then, faced with so much remembering, can an individual hope to establish a consensus memory? And if a consensus memory is impossible, is the counsel of despair just quoted the only possible attitude?

The new hermeneutics of history asks us to make room for excess, for the uncountable, but at the same time to re-negotiate our position with an absence, with ignorance. As Vilém Flusser points out, we live in a world in which information slowly unravels and disperses, according to the second law of thermodynamics.[21] Mankind resists this natural entropy by storing and transmitting information. This is one of the principal tasks assigned to photography from the outset; this is the task that objects have in the junk-shop. However, despite photographic museums, collections, albums, photography has itself become the instrument of this informational entropy. This is partly because, for the family snapper, what is stored is not the negative, but a single, vulnerable, positive print. And it is partly because, even though photographic archives exist, their coherence and efficacy depend on systems of classification that might tend to defeat recuperation. Archives, paradoxically, are about the disappearance of photographs and about the failure of classification. Where would you put a photo of a picnic in Scotland in 1943? Under picnics? Scottish family life? The home front in 1943? And anyway, how do I know I am looking for it? Knowledge is created by coincidence. The new Biblothèque Nationale is Sebald's example of this archival dysfunction.[22]

Besides, unlike painting, photography must, in order to *make* its image, actively *exclude* what does not enter the frame. Thus, in order to give knowledge, the photograph must, equally and oppositely, create an ignorance. Of course it tries to persuade us to forget this, to persuade us that what is taking place in the frame is *all* that is taking place. But the excluded blind field is only waiting its moment to return and haunt us. And, with so many new photographs being taken every instant, any photograph of anything may come to light at any time and potentially change our assessment of reality. Photographs are vulnerable, fragile objects and most of them are hidden from view. But we, by the same token, are vulnerable to photos, to their sudden emergences from the shadows, to shake the known world and put a different complexion on it. What, too, of all the photographs that are not taken?[23] The only reasonable position is infinitely to postpone the drawing of the historical map, even though one's narrative is driven by the very need to.

Ignorance is an existential condition rather than a quantitative or statistical one. To know what one does not know is a healthy spur to find out. But that, erroneously, is to imply that ignorance itself is a measurable and finite thing. In fact, we do not know how much we do not know. The more we discover, the more, proportionately, our ignorance increases; the more we do not know, the more injustices we do, the more we misrepresent reality, the more prejudiced we are, the more unjustified is the store we put by what we *do* know, the photographs we *do* have. Sebald's photos do not fill holes, they create them. We must, then, write the kind of history in which we not only take responsibility for our ignorance, but acknowledge that it is a guilt that subsumes all others, and that is always in excess of memory's capacity to redeem it.

Knowledge of a photograph, or a junk-shop object, lies in our ability to penetrate, to reconstruct, its blind field (*hors champ*). The blind field calls forth the language of narrative and makes the photograph (image-object) a metonymy: [24] across its frame it expands into the synchronicity and diachronicity of space and time (the text in which it is set). A narrator makes a frame permeable, maintains the image's indexicality, makes it the servant of its own, single narrative. With the passage of time and the loss of narrators, the frame of the photograph hardens, or, put another way, it becomes a unit of enumeration, and the image aspires to a certain (aesthetic?) self-sufficiency beyond indexicality; its metonymic value is thrown into question. Alternatively, the frame falls away and the image's indexicality floats and warps, so that it can indulge in temporal and spatial promiscuity.

If the frame hardens, the photograph becomes peculiarly available to the person unfamiliar with it: its optical unconscious is released. Benjamin's account of the optical unconscious[25] might lead one to believe that it derives from the camera's prosthetic technology (instantaneousness, time-lapse, enlargement), but Barthes's *punctum*[26] is also a manifestation of the optical unconscious: we are 'pricked' by something in a photograph which does not belong to us and yet which takes us somewhere deep into our own existence (trauma, repressed desire or fantasy, involuntary memory). Our own photos provide only instances of voluntary memory, partial recoveries of the past, slivers of factual autobiography; but other people's photos *may* trigger involuntary memories that reach into the duration of our *moi profond* (fictional, unconscious) and expand into our own lost worlds.

If the frame dissolves, on the other hand, then the image has a new set of options on the world, and joins the community of the achronological and the aspatial, creates cross-temporal and cross-spatial correspondences. In terms of narrative structure, the dissolution of the frame entails the abandonment of the paragraph, as we begin to discover in *Die Ringe des Saturn*, and as we find it accomplished in *Austerlitz*. The junk-shop owner is not the once-and-for-all historian of his possessions, but the (commercial) engineer, by buying and selling, of their endlessly permutative relationships.

This view of the dissolving frame involves some disagreement with Sebald's own account of the function of photographs within his work. In an interview with Eleanor Wachtel, Sebald identifies two purposes in his use of photographs: first, that of verification, and:

> The other function that I see is possibly that of arresting time. Fiction is an art form that moves in time, that is inclined towards the end, that works on a negative gradient, and it is very, very difficult in that particular form in the narrative to arrest the passage of time. And as we all know, this is what we like so much about certain forms of visual art – you stand in a museum and you look at one of those wonderful pictures somebody did in the sixteenth or the eighteenth century. You are taken out of time, and that is in a sense a form of redemption, if you can release yourself from time. And the photographs can also do this – they act like barriers or weirs which stem the flow [27]

Not only does this view seem dangerously to blend the notions of arrested time and being outside time, but it is a view which seems to run counter to two other propositions that Sebald wants to make: that the photographs have a power of authentication (ninety percent are authentic by his own calculation,[28] (but see argument below)), and that they are the occasion of the spectral return of their subjects. Rather than 'arrests time', it would be more accurate to say that the photograph 'makes contact with time in an instant of its passing', but is also carried forward in that passing. The photograph then constantly re-surfaces in time. The very arythmia of the photographs' appearance in the text captures the randomness of their advent, of their re-entry into narratorial time; photographs, like enumerated objects, are coincidences, and, consequently, they as much make chance out of destiny, as destiny out of chance. One might thus also say that they do not arrest time so much as diversify and re-project it, by means of their momentary suspensions. These suspensions allow Sebald's text to move freely backwards and forwards in time, so that we lose our temporal bearings and enter the labyrinth that is our re-education in the making of History. The 'time' of the photograph is the present participle, a part of speech which itself is no tense, but can attach itself to any tense. There are already intimations of this condition at Somerleyton, thanks to the enumerated objects: 'Nor can one readily say which decade or century it is, for many ages are superimposed here and coexist.'[29]

A passage in *Austerlitz* reminds us that enumeration is also and equally the world of elasticized space, offering alternative geographical patchworks:

> My mind thus gradually created a kind of ideal landscape in which the Arabian desert, the realm of the Aztecs, the continent of Antarctica, the snow-covered Alps, the North-West Passage, the river Congo and the Crimean peninsula formed a single panorama, populated by all the figures proper to those places.[30]

At any time in the school day at Stower Grange, Austerlitz is free to move into this improbable landscape and thus avoid the depression that afflicts so many of the boys. Even as enumeration enacts dispersal and separation, it makes available the endless possibilities of reconfiguration. Parataxis is both the syntax of static juxtaposition and the syntax of redisposability and undefined relationality. Gravitation and levitation are bound in an inextricable embrace.

What we then might argue is that the indexical value of the Sebaldian photograph is weakened in favour of its transferability, of its lack of resistance to illusion and hallucination and uncertainty; photographs float more freely, less self-assertively. And, correspondingly, they begin to occupy a position closer to the borderline between the real and the imaginary, the literal and figurative, the actual/past and the possible/future. The photograph, then, far from persisting obstinately in its own moment, becomes a 'shifter', whose temporal and spatial specificity, like that of deictics,[31] can be infinitely redefined in relation to the person who looks. Photographs are less important for what they depict than for the uses to which they are put in an individual consciousness. This malleable transferability relative to spectatorial position corresponds to the transferability of narrators (e.g. Lucy Landau, William Hazel, Frederick Farrar, Luisa Lanzberg). In such a world, Nabokov has no problem standing in for Henry Selwyn.

If, then, History as a teleology of knowledge must be abandoned, even though narratives are driven by the urgent need to pursue it; if that pursuit is so dispersed that it becomes, to all intents and purposes, an indefatigable prevarication, then what does 'historical' writing become? Crudely put, History surrenders to historicity, is entirely to be found in the motion of the writing hand/narrating voice which is the very embodiment of consciousness unfolding in real time. But the unfolding of consciousness is not linear, but ramifying, rhizomatic, constantly converting chronometric time into a flexible inner duration.

This kind of enumeration affirms the spirit of the eccentric, embodied, for instance, in the figure of George Wyndham Le Strange, whose enumerated habits [32] are a release into the unruly and inconsequential, allowing him to live on the periphery, in the tangential, beyond the fixations of the *con*centric. From the torment of the circles of hell, or of the *unicursal* labyrinth (Breendonk, with Améry's torture-chamber as its destinational centre), one is liberated into the non-tendentious of the *multicursal* labyrinth, into an unending prevarication, or what one might term a willing imprisonment in tireless fascination. Austerlitz must go on looking for his father, but in the reassuring knowledge that he will not find him.

The enumerative principle belongs as much to the artist's studio as to the junk shop, inasmuch as it is a place of collection, an archive, of the artist's materials, on the one hand, and *objets trouvés*, props for the next canvas, on the other. One of the studio's manifestations is as a place of transformation: the capacity to redeem, and resurrect to new activity, objects and materials which have lapsed into neglect or inertial oblivion, depends on the artist's ability to reinvent his own position, from that of habitual occupier of the studio to that of its discoverer as a cave of wonders. And this, in turn, involves the fostering of a mobile consciousness, a constant relativisation of the viewing position.

There are precious few literal artists' studios in Sebald's work, but one environment that is acted upon in the creative way just described is the emporium of Paul Bereyter's father, Theodor, and the vision of it generated by Paul himself:

> [Theodor] sold everything in the emporium, from coffee to collar studs, camisoles to cuckoo clocks, candied sugar to collapsible top hats.[33]

As a child, Paul rides through the emporium on his tricycle, his diminutive size turning the gangways into ravines and reducing the light available from the high, small transom windows, so that smell projects some goods more vividly than others: 'mothballs and lily-of-the-valley soap were always the most pungent, while felted wool and loden cloth assailed the nose only in wet weather, herrings and linseed oil in hot'.[34] 'For hours on end, Paul had said, deeply moved by his own memories, he had ridden in those days past the dark rows of bolts of materials, the gleaming leather boots, the preserve jars, the galvanized watering cans, the whip stand, and the case that seemed especially magical to him, in which rolls of Gütermann's sewing thread were neatly arranged behind little glass windows, in every colour of the rainbow.'[35] Paul's stature and mobility are the key to an inexhaustible relativisation of position, to a perceptual eccentricity, which recomposes, with unending variations, the goods on display, producing a syntax which naturally feels exploratory and full of patient stamina.

Michael Hulse's translation of this passage maintains the alliteration on /k/ which marks the enumeration of items in the German: '[...] ein Emporium, in dem es alles zu kaufen gab vom Bohnenkaffee bis zum Kragenknopf, vom Kamisol bis zur Kuckucksuhr und vom Kandiszucker bis zum Klappzylinder'.[36] But what his translation cannot capture is the longer string of /k/, which includes the /k/ of the emporium's blind field: ein kultivierter Melancholiker, Kramladen, Kind, Kaufmannslehre, Kapital, Kinderzeit, seiner geringen Körpergröße,

Kind. The objects in the emporium thus fall into a design constituted of culture, commerce and childhood, as if alliteration could see not only the objects but their larger ramifications. Alliteration itself is, of course, an enumerative mechanism, but one woven into the very fabric of hypotaxis. And we should not perhaps think of alliteration in these circumstances as a stylistic device, as an intended effect, but as a natural concomitant of hypotaxis, its other face, a paratactic, junk-shop 'syntax', in which enumeration discovers its true energies, the energies of progressive modulation, metamorphosis, assimilability, levitation.

The gravitational model of studio experience is much grimmer. While goods in the emporium seem susceptible of any number of dynamic reconfigurations thanks to the mobile viewing subject, it is the goods themselves which are on the move in Ferber's studio and he himself the inert object. This is the dystopian aspect of the animism of objects:

> The darkness that had gathered in the corners, the puffy tidemarked plaster and the paint that flaked off the walls, the shelves overloaded with books and piles of newspapers, the boxes, work benches and side tables, the wing armchair, the gas cooker, the mattresses, the crammed mountains of papers, crockery and various materials, the paint pots gleaming carmine red, leaf green and lead white in the gloom, the blue flames of the two paraffin heaters: the entire furniture was advancing, millimeter by millimeter, upon the central space where Ferber had set up his easel in the grey light that entered through a high north-facing window layered with the dust of decades.[37]

The enumerated objects here indulge in an imperceptible centripetal or concentric movement, which one feels will smother Ferber, or reduce him to the pile of dust over which he presides. Ferber's studio is not a studio of transformation, but one of confrontation: the artist, confined to the studio, confronts, and is confronted by, his own materials (including the human model) and, through them, by his art, his creativity. But Ferber's art is generated and paralysed by the palimpsestic sedimentation of previous images.[38] The work of art may, like the photograph, be the home of ancestral ghosts; but those who return, the revenants, may as easily suffocate the viewer as intrigue him.

We know that the narrator himself is subject to the Ferberian condition; he tells us:

> Often I could not get on for hours or days at a time, and not infrequently I unraveled what I had done, continuously tormented by scruples that were taking tighter hold and steadily paralyzing me. […] I had covered hundreds of pages with my scribble, in pencil and ballpoint. By far the greater part had been crossed out, discarded, or obliterated by additions. Even what I ultimately salvaged as a 'final' version seemed to me a thing of shreds and patches, utterly botched.[39]

But we remember those equal and opposite words from 'All'estero' (*Vertigo*), cited in footnote 18. And we remember, too, the junk shop in Terezín, ANTIKOS BAZAR, identified in the German as a 'Magazin' (storeroom), but translated appropriately by Michael Hulse as 'emporium', given what we have said of the emporium of Paul Bereyter's father, Theodor, and given the vast dimensions of this junk-shop, which make it a distillation of a whole world of objects become enumeration: 'Es nimmt die ganze Vorderfront eines der größten Häuser ein und geht, glaube ich, auch weit in die Tiefe'[40] [It occupies the entire façade of one of the largest buildings, and I think its vaults reach back a long way as well[41]]. If 'Auflösung' is the term of a potential, triumphant reversal, so enumerated objects, as we have seen, have the power to turn the tables. It is not the objects in the ANTIKOS BAZAR that are felt to be the revenants, the phantoms of the past, but the lime trees of the square and the narrator himself whose 'own faint shadow image' is 'barely perceptible among them'.[42] By virtue of what do these objects enter into re-possession of their kingdom, into the exertion of a mesmerizing influence? By virtue of their mooted power to provide answers: 'as if one of them or their relationship with each other must provide an unequivocal answer to the many questions I found it impossible to ask in mind'.[43] By virtue of their being, like the river on the painted lampshade running through Bohemia or Brazil, without origin or destination, but always flowing back into itself:[44] in the end, like these objects, photographs, too, enter an indeterminate space without origin or objective, as if merely replenishing themselves with the very passage of time, ever re-absorbing their changing context, ever being re-digested by their spectators.

Photographs implicate us. In Jérôme Thélot's terms, the photograph's ability to create an obligation in the spectator is 'anticipation d'une rétrospection, prévoyance d'une nostalgie, prévision d'un souvenir' [anticipation of a retrospection, the foreseeing of a nostalgia, the prediction of a memory].[45] But, if anything, these words put too much emphasis on the retrospective: photographs are always catching up with us, indeed may seem already to have taken us into account, to have more knowledge than we have. And sometimes, conversely, we may seem to rescue them (see footnote 4). But our obligation to them cannot be collectively redeemed, because neither the subject of the picture nor the spectator knows exactly what obligation has been generated, what kind of moral pressure has been exerted. Moral obligations of this kind become increasingly subjective. If someone could write a reliable, objective history of these photographs then we would all be saved. Unfortunately, history and memory are not the same thing, any more than history and association are.

Sebald says, as already reported, that one purpose of the photographs in his work is that of verification. But we should be wary of attributing an authenticating capacity to these photographs, for three principal reasons. First, critics are agreed about the modest picture quality, and Sebald is only too ready to agree: 'I don't want to integrate images of high photographic quality into my texts; they are rather documents of findings, something secondary. It is actually quite nice when this indistinctness somehow finds its way into the images.'[46] If sharpness of focus is a sine qua non of truth claims, and if instantaneousness is what guarantees the sense of immediacy of contact with the subject, then we would say that Sebald's photographs have no interest in either.

Secondly, many of the photographs, in their taking, apparently post-date the event that is their subject: they are taken expressly in order to give proof of, to bear witness to, that event (as, say, the photographs of Orfordness, or of the Breendonk fortifications). Many other photographs are encountered, are already in existence; they have to be accounted for, given meaning, placed. But in the relation between photograph and text, the photograph, like the enumerated object, *always predates the text*, even where, in the chronology of events, they postdate it. A photograph predates text because the photograph is a primary material, a raw material, in a way that writing cannot be, because the indexical of image predates the symbolic of language. How else does Helen Hollaender get into Paul Bereyter's narrative, if not abruptly, without narrative preparation, from the sudden emergence of photographs of her? Writing about a photograph is either tautological – the finest example of which is the textual repetition of Ambros Adelwarth's photographed note that he has gone to Ithaca – [47] or it takes place as the image's blind field. Writing is always too late. Photographs cannot be called upon to authenticate writing.

The third reason concerns the status of the photographs themselves: in truth, these are photographic reproductions (as Sebald puts it: 'documents of findings') or reproduced photographs (with all that is implied of possible interference), rather than photographs. And many of them are already second-hand, that is, postcards, the circumstances of whose taking have been occluded and which already have on them a printed caption. What possible authenticating value can a postcard have? [48]

It is not, therefore, the authenticating power of these photographs that we should pursue, their ability to establish History, even if only in a fragmentary way. History is perspectival; its objective is a vanishing point which puts everything this side of the horizon in place, immobilizes it, makes it measurable, and at the same time immobilizes the spectator, insists that he/she stays in a privileged viewing position. Sebald's syntax, whether, in the end, we speak of his hypotaxis, or of the parataxis of enumerated objects and photographs by which it is intimately inhabited, is an experience of the planar, that is to say, of a mobile point of view engaged in constantly shifting encounters with elements of the landscape, never reaching the horizon. In this world, the long view is as confusing as the close-up. But at the same time, gravitation may be released into levitation: photographs, for example, which may seem to be a record of outer events become the inventors of inner events, or indeed of new facts. History is displaced to reveal either histories or historicity, not a perspective on time but an engagement with time. It is only in the displacements of Historical authenticity that authentic experience becomes available.

1 Sir Thomas Browne, *Selected Writings*, ed. Claire Preston (Manchester, Carcanet Press: 2003), p.34.
2 'In common with other English writers of the seventeenth century, Browne wrote out of the fullness of his erudition, deploying a vast repertoire of quotations and the names of authorities who had gone before, creating complex metaphors and analogies, and constructing labyrinthine sentences that sometimes extend over one or two pages, sentences that resemble processions or a funeral cortège in their sheer ceremonial lavishness. It is true that, because of the immense weight of the impediments he is carrying, Browne's writing can be held back by the force of gravitation, but when he does succeed in rising higher and higher through the circles of his spiralling prose, borne aloft like a glider on warm currents of air, even today the reader is overcome by a sense of levitation. The greater the distance the clearer the view: one sees the tiniest of details with the utmost clarity. It is as if one were looking through a reversed opera glass and through a microscope at the same time'. *The Rings of Saturn*, trans. Michael Hulse (London, Harvill/Vintage: 2002), p.19.
3 Michael Silverblatt in conversation with Sebald in 'A Poem of an Invisible Subject', *The Emergence of Memory: Conversations with W.G. Sebald*. Ed. Lynne Sharon Swartz (New York: Seven Stories, 2007), pp.77-8. 'Hypotaxis' describes a syntax of intricate embeddings and subordinations. Its antonym, 'parataxis', shortly to appear, describes a syntax of consecutive main clauses, or the non-hierarchic itemization of nouns.
4 'For many years I have found images in a most unsystematic manner. One finds such things enclosed in old books that one buys. One finds them in antique shops or thrift shops. That's typical for photographs after all, that they lead such a nomadic existence and then are "rescued" by someone.' Christian Scholz in conversation with Sebald in '"But the Written Word is Not a True Document": A Conversation with W.G. Sebald on Literature and Photography' *Searching for Sebald: Photography after W.G. Sebald*. Ed. Lise Patt (ed.) with Christel Dillbohner (Los Angeles, Institute of Critical Enquiry: 2007), pp.542-9; p.546.
5 J.J. Long *W.G. Sebald – Image, Archive, Modernity* (Edinburgh, Edinburgh University Press: 2007).
6 *The Rings of Saturn*, p.36.
7 *Schwindel. Gefühle.* (Frankfurt am Main, Eichborn Verlag: 1990). Published in English as *Vertigo*, trans. Michael Hulse (London, Harvill/Vintage: 2002).
8 *Schwindel. Gefühle.*, p.254.
9 *Vertigo*, pp. 223-4.
10 *Schwindel. Gefühle.*, p.257.
11 *Vertigo*, p.226.
12 *Schwindel. Gefühle.*, p.254.
13 *Vertigo*, p.224
14 *Schwindel. Gefühle.*, p.252.
15 *Vertigo*, p. 222
16 Deane Blackler *Reading W.G. Sebald: Adventure and Disobedience* (Rochester NY, Camden House: 2007), p. 28.
17 Jean-Christophe Bailly *L'Instant et son ombre*: Essai (Paris, Seuil: 2008), p.124.
18 This will remind us of the narrator's description of his own practice, in 'All'estero' (*Vertigo*, p.94): 'I sat at a table near the open terrace door, my papers and notes spread out around me, drawing connections between events that lay far apart but which seemed to me to be of the same order.'
19 The 'indexicality' of a photograph refers to the necessary co-presence of subject and camera at the moment of its taking; the camera captures the light directly projected from the subject, which makes paramount the photograph's referential value. This notion might be applied to the enumerated object, as a necessary relationship between the object and its (original) environment, a relationship which time undoes, until the object has to sacrifice its 'true' environment for the arbitrary

environment of the second-hand shop or auction room.
20 *Vertigo*, p.212.
21 Vilém Flusser *Pour une philosophie de la photographie*, trans. Jean Mouchard (Paris, Circé: 1996), p.53.
22 *Austerlitz*, trans. Anthea Bell (London, Hamish Hamilton: 2001), pp.392-3.
23 *Austerlitz* (Munich, Carl Hanser Verlag: 2001), pp. 90; 127; 129.
24 'Metonymy' is the designation of a whole by one of its parts; the naming of the part presupposes the recuperation of the whole.
25 Alan Trachtenberg (ed), *Classic Essays on Photography*. Notes by Amy Weinstein Meyers. (New Haven CN, Leete's Island Books: 1980), pp.202-3.
26 Roland Barthes, *Camera Lucida: Reflections on Photography*, trans. Richard Howard (London, Vintage: 2000), pp. 25-7.
27 Sebald in conversation with Eleanor Wachtel in 'Ghost Hunter', *The Emergence of Memory* pp. 37-61; pp. 41-2. Sebald endorses this ('Grecian urn') view of arrested time in *Austerlitz*, in the objects of the ANTIKOS BAZAR in Terezín, which are likened to a porcelain group of a horseman saving a girl in distress: 'They were all as timeless [zeitlos] as that moment of rescue, perpetuated [verewigte] but for ever just occurring [sich ereignende], [...]'. *Austerlitz* (London), pp.276-7.
28 *Ibid.*, p.41.
29 *The Rings of Saturn*, p. 36.
30 *Austerlitz* (London), p.85.
31 'Deictics' are words which relate an utterance to a time, place or person (e.g. adverbs (tomorrow, in this house), pronouns (I, she, him)) and whose reference changes relative to the speaker or writer; because of this relativity of reference, they have also been called 'shifters'. See, e.g., Roman Jakobson, *Shifters, Verbal Categories and the Russian Verb* (Cambridge MA, Harvard UP: 1957).
32 *The Rings of Saturn*, pp. 62-4.
33 *The Emigrants*, trans. Michael Hulse (London, Harvill/Vintage: 2002), p.51.
34 *Ibid.*, p.51.
35 *Ibid.*, pp.51-2.
36 *Die Ausgewanderten* (Frankfurt am Main, Eichborn Verlag: 1992), p.75.
37 *The Emigrants*, pp.160-1.
38 '[...] and if he then decided that the portrait was done, not so much because he was convinced that it was finished as through sheer exhaustion, an onlooker might well feel that it had evolved from a long lineage of grey, ancestral faces, rendered unto ash but still there, as ghostly presences, on the harried paper'. *The Emigrants*, p. 162.
39 *The Emigrants*, pp. 230-1.
40 *Austerlitz* (Munich), p.278.
41 *Austerlitz* (London), p.273
42 *Ibid.*, p.277.
43 *Ibid.*, pp.274-5.
44 *Ibid.*, p.276
45 Jérôme Thélot, *Critique de la raison photographique* (Paris, Éditions Les Belles Lettres: 2009), p.117.
46 'But the Written Word is Not a True Document', p.106.
47 *The Emigrants*, p.103.
48 Long draws our attention to the large collection of postcards gathered by the landlady of the Engelwirt, Rosina Zobel, and remarks: 'It is not only that the experience of place is mediated by the image, but that all places lose their geographical specificity and subjective significance once they are mass-produced in postcard format, enter the space of commodity circulation, and are enshrined within the pages of the album.' *W.G. Sebald – Image, Archive, Modernity*, pp.65-6.

Tess Jaray

*

Two Pieces

1. *I borrowed it from Kafka*, or A pool of frozen water

It's now thirteen years since Max died and I wonder if it's possible that memories, by their very nature, can be painful – after all, we are certainly all condemned to nostalgia – even if the events recalled were not. And in his case death was so unexpected, so violent, that other things are overshadowed.

But meeting Max, under any circumstances, is not something easily forgotten. He had a penetrating presence, even when silent. Perhaps most when silent. He was inclined to confessional mode, I suspect. Is that perhaps a particularly German trait? He seemed to have deliberately jettisoned some German qualities: he was self-deprecating, which the English are so good at. In other words, if you say you don't know anything about a particular subject, you're covered both ways. If caught out, there is always the 'I told you so', and if you prove to be the world's greatest expert, how nicely modest you appear.

Much to be said for the famous English hypocrisy, and he was in favour of it.

But push him a little further and truth slipped out – as with his hilarity when he saw that the eminent Professors who came to UEA to validate his department brought their wives with them – 'because there was a pool in the hotel…' He did also have a great admiration for Thomas Bernhardt.

Anyone familiar with Max's writing knows that this was not a tranquil man, but someone who was at times almost incapacitated by the horrors of the world. I remember one of the very first occasions when we met, he was standing by the window in my studio. It was morning and the room was flooded with light and the reflected colours of the paintings on the walls. I don't know what happened – or indeed what I may have said – but I looked at him standing there and thought, this man has turned into a block of ice. Later, a year or two on, he sent me the just published *Austerlitz*. And when I reached page 303, I read the following: 'When we wake up tomorrow, she said, I shall wish you every happiness, and it will be like telling a machine working by some unknown mechanism that I hope it will run well. Can't you tell me the reason, she asked, said Austerlitz, why you remain so unapproachable? Why, she said, have you been like a pool of frozen water ever since we came here...'[1]

I recognized exactly – exactly – how someone else had seen that in him, and that he too must have recognized that truth, and recorded it.

And I was startled, too, by how much more beautiful the expression 'pool of water' was than my rather banal image of 'a block of ice'.

Before he saw the prints I was in the process of making, each one to relate to a text taken from *The Rings of Saturn* and *Vertigo*, I sent him the extracts that I hoped to use. He approved all of them, except one, which I had thought strangely powerful in its darkness, and which described, in *The Rings of Saturn*, the moments outside Michael and Anne Hamburger's house: 'We waited for the taxi beside the Hölderlin pump, and by the faint light that fell from the living room window into the well I saw, with a shudder that went to the roots of my hair, a beetle rowing across the surface of the water, from one dark shore to another.'[2] 'This', he said, 'I'm afraid you can't have, as I borrowed it from Kafka.'

Later, he looked at the prints I had pinned up in the studio – there were eighteen pairs, each one an image relating, in my mind, to an extrapolated text from either *The Rings of Saturn* or *Vertigo*. He looked at them slowly, for a long time, his attitude a mixture of mildness and concentration. And he really looked. Really looked. This is a very rare and wonderful quality in someone who is not a visual artist, and greatly valued by painters. He said they were 'weightless', which no one had ever done before, and to me is exact.

And when, some time later, we were talking about making a book together with some tiny poems he would write, he wrote to me, 'I can imagine that because of their diminutive size and oblique nature they would go well with your weightless pictures.'

What he didn't know was that the word 'oblique', which no one had used either, was not only exact, but perfect.

Max died before we could speak about the publication of the little book, and it is very sad to see – after some ten years – that his last letter to me ended with the words ... 'The wisdom of old age is lacking sorely...'

Max Sebald at Advanced Graphics, with Tess Jaray's images from *The Rings of Saturn and Vertigo* 2001, photograph: Cameron Lindo

2. A mystery and a confession

On Tuesday, 21st March 2000, I met with W.G.Sebald to discuss the project I was then working on – a series of brightly coloured screen-prints that had been conceived in relation to selected extracts from his books *The Rings of Saturn* and *Vertigo*.

Having gained his approval of the texts, and his interest in the rather poor snapshots of the process of making the work – shots of my studio, the graphics studio, and some general views of the images as they were developing – I was encouraged enough to tell him that I also had in mind an 'artist's book' that I would love to do in relation to his verse, if he had any he would consider letting me have. He reached into a drawer and handed me a long poem – 'prose poem' is probably the correct way to describe it – written in German; and said, see what you make of this.

On the train home the next day I read it. Several times. Although I speak German only very badly and would be neither qualified nor able to describe it with justice, I could see that it had that same wonderful voice that his books have – and I was again bewitched by the language. It had twenty-three stanzas, and told how he, Sebald/The Poet, had been in Marienbad; and had there so clearly imagined the Famous Poet who had been there before him. How long before was not explained, but references to the poet's journey home by coach and over a mountain range suggested at least a hundred, perhaps two hundred years, or longer. As did his description of the way in which the Famous Poet proposes marriage to his beloved, through her mother; how after being refused, he departs in sombre mood; and how he wrote, on that coach, the famous twenty-three stanza elegy, which he, the Famous Poet, would later say was the most mature creation of his old age.

Sebald/the Poet then goes on to describe how he can't quite take to the work, and was in fact far more intrigued by mementos of the Poet's beloved Ulrike on display in the museum there, among other things from the period; and how these were the objects that made the deepest impression on him.

Who was the poet? Who was the girl? It seemed imperative to know, as in a thriller. The two or three people who might have helped me I didn't want to ask; and my father, who would have known immediately, was dead.

I pondered this interesting problem, but being on a train there wasn't much I could do about it. When I got home I knew I had to find a translator – fast – since I was leaving for the country in two days to look after my sister's cats and to sort out some correspondence between our grandparents and parents that had recently been found, dating from Vienna in the late 1930s and early 1940s. I found someone immediately, a German student who enjoyed translating poetry, and, even better, did not know Sebald's work.

On the train again, this time to Worcestershire, I studied the poem once more – but now in English. In spite of obvious mistakes, and perhaps because I had asked her to do it straight, not making an art of it, the voice came across – slow, clear, and with a powerful erotic force.

Who was this poet from centuries ago?

When I arrived I unpacked and fed the cats. The house is quite isolated, with the garden banked up in front, the camelias almost obscenely profuse. The silence is as profound as you get in England, just some cattle and the occasional bird calling. I went to my bedroom, which used to be my father's, and looked at his bookshelves. There are just a few hundred books, which my parents brought from Vienna, mostly the German classics, with some Russian and some French.

I looked at the thirty-odd volumes of Goethe on the top shelf, but discarded the thought. He had been happy in his old age, so wasn't a contender, was he?

On the shelf below there were four volumes by Schiller. I took down the last one, which presumably would have been the late work. There were three periods, and I turned to the last again, Die Dritte Period. There it was, the twenty-three stanza work, *Die Kraniche des Ibykus* (The Cranes of Ibykus), a military poem. In my memory it seems to have opened at that page. In Gothic script, of course, which was way beyond me.

At that moment a friend telephoned me, someone who knew about these things. I asked: do you know *Die Kraniche des Ibykus*? Who doesn't, came the answer, to which I might have replied, there may be just a few English people left who don't.

Two days later my sister returned, and started playing with her new computer. Look up Schiller in Marienbad on the Internet, I asked her, and there it was, Schiller in Marianbad, Schiller in Marienbad, Schiller in Marienbad – three times, three different books.

Had I found the poet and his sad love? And who was Ibykus? I still didn't know if Sebald/the Poet had set me a fearful intelligence test, which I had probably failed. But something was at work, and even intuition didn't seem to be quite the right word for it.

The mystery went on. Katia, another phone friend, being an inveterate researcher, found out that night who Ibykus was. From (in turn) an obsessively learned friend who insisted he had first to read Sebald in the original German. Ibykus was, of course, a poet. From ancient Greece. So we have the poet writing about a poet writing about a poet. Not only a thriller, but a labyrinth. And how wonderful that Sebald/The Poet admits in his elegy that he couldn't quite take to the poem. Even (or perhaps particularly) in German, its grandeur is not for us now. It made me laugh, although I could hear the shocked shadows from the past. But why ancient Greece? What did military conquests have to do with love? And there were eight lines in each stanza, but only six in the elegy by Sebald/the Poet. I couldn't imagine him ever leaving loose ends.

So I still fretted. Why would Sebald/the Poet have referred to the Famous Poet's having written this in his old age – Seines Alters, he writes – when Schiller was only in his mid-forties when he died? Even in the mid-eighteenth century that was not yet old. And so when my friend Anne called me two days later and said, I told you so: it wasn't Schiller it was Goethe; he was famously at Marienbad, and the poem was the even more famous *Trilogie der Leidenschaft* (Trilogy of Passion) – I was not only grateful to be saved humiliation but immediately forgave her for knowing so much more than I do.

But this thread had not quite unravelled because, to my amazement, I soon caught sight of a book I had brought back with me from the country. Eckermann's *Gesprache mit Goethe* (Conversations with Goethe), a beautiful edition printed in 1921, and illustrated with foxed plates of the great poet's life. There, on page 607, in clear Gothic script, was Goethe's discussion of his elegy. Now, it seemed,

I had to wait. But I couldn't wait. Never could. So I try Waterstone's in Camden Town, who had never heard of Goethe. And then I tried Compendium, which had only one volume of the Famous Poet's works. But there the poem was, clear and legible, with a straight prose translation. Twenty-three stanzas, each with six lines. Not twenty-three stanzas with eight lines each, like Schiller's *Ibykus*.

And now there is only one mystery left. Did Sebald/the Poet write it because he too experienced love in Marienbad?

I think we will never know, and I think we are not meant to.

[1] *Austerlitz*, p 303
[2] *The Rings of Saturn*, p 190

Overleaf: *Requiem Blue* Tess Jaray 2002

*

Select Bibliography

This bibliography lists the main works of W.G. Sebald in order of their English, UK publication. Publication details for the first German editions are also given.

The Emigrants, trans. Michael Hulse (London, The Harvill Press: 1996)
[*Die Ausgewanderten: Vier lange Erzahlungen* (Frankfurt a.M., Eichborn: 1992)]
The Rings of Saturn, trans. Michael Hulse (London, The Harvill Press: 1998)
[*Die Ringe des Saturn: Eine englische Wallfahrt* (Frankfurt a.M., Eichborn:1995)]
Vertigo, trans. Michael Hulse (London, The Harvill Press: 1999)
[*Schwindel. Gefuhle.* (Franfurt a.M., Eichborn: 1990)]
Austerlitz, trans. Anthea Bell (London, Hamish Hamilton: 2001)
[*Austerlitz* (Munich and Vienna, Carl Hanser: 2001)]
For Years Now: Poems. Images by Tess Jaray (London, Short Books: 2001)
After Nature, trans. Michael Hamburger (London, Hamish Hamilton: 2002)
[*Nach der Natur: Ein Elementargedicht. Photographien von Thomas Becker* (Nordlingen, Franz Greno: 1988)]
On the Natural History of Destruction. With Essays on Alfred Andersch, Jean Amery and Peter Weiss, trans. Anthea Bell (London, Hamish Hamilton: 2003)
[*Luftkrieg und Literatur. Mit einem Essay zu Alfred Andersch* (Munich and Vienna, Carl Hanser: 1999)]

Unrecounted: 33 Poems, with Jan Peter Tripp, trans. Michael Hamburger
   (London, Hamish Hamilton: 2004)
[*Unerzahlt; 33 Texte und 33 Radierungen* (Munich and Vienna, Carl
   Hanser: 2003)]
Campo Santo, trans. Anthea Bell (London, Hamish Hamilton: 2005)
[*Campo Santo*, ed. Sven Meyer (Munich and Vienna, Carl Hanser: 2003)]
Across the Land and the Water: Selected Poems, 1964-2001, trans. Iain
   Galbraith (London, Hamish Hamilton: 2011)
[*Uber das Land und das Wasser: Ausgewahlte Gedichte 1964-2001* (Munich
   and Vienna, Carl Hanser: 2008)]
*A Place in the Country: on Gottfried Keller, Johann Peter Hebel, Robert
   Walser and Others*, trans. Jo Catling (London, Hamish Hamilton: 2013)
[*Logis in einem Landhaus: Uber Gottfried Keller, Johann Peter Hebel, Robert
   Walser und andere* (Munich and Vienna, Carl Hanser: 1998)]

※

Authors

Dame Gillian Beer was the King Edward VII Professor of English Literature at the University of Cambridge until her retirement. More recently she has been the Andrew Mellon Senior Scholar at the Yale Center for British Art, 2009-2011. Her books include *Darwin's Plots* (3rd edition 2009), *Open Fields: Science in Cultural Encounter* (1996), *Virginia Woolf: the Common Ground* (1996) and *Jabberwocky and Other Nonsense: the collected and annotated poems of Lewis Carroll* (2012).

Jon Cook is a Professor of Literature at the University of East Anglia. His recent publications include *Poetry in Theory* and *Hazlitt in Love*.

Tacita Dean was born in 1965 in Canterbury, UK. She studied at Falmouth School of Art and the Slade School of Fine Art before moving to Berlin on a DAAD scholarship in 2000 where she continues to live and work.

Tess Jaray is a painter who also writes. She has exhibited nationally and internationally, and has work in public collections including the Tate Gallery, the Arts Council and the British Museum. A monograph on her work was published by Ridinghouse in early 2014. Her latest book, *The Blue Cupboard*, which includes a short piece on Sebald, was published by RA Publishing in October 2014.

Richard Long is acknowledged worldwide as one of Britain's leading contemporary artists. He was born in Bristol in 1945 and represented Britain at the 1976 Venice Biennale. He was awarded the Turner Prize in 1989.

Robert Macfarlane is the author of a trilogy of books about landscape and imagination, *Mountains of the Mind* (2003), *The Wild Places* (2007) and *The Old Ways* (2012). He is a Fellow of Emmanuel College, Cambridge.

Will Self is the author of many novels, short story collections, and works of non-fiction. He is a prolific journalist and a regular broadcaster on radio and television. He is also Professor of Contemporary Thought at Brunel University. He lives in south London.

Ali Smith lives in Cambridge. Her latest novel is *How to be both*, Hamish Hamilton (2014).

Clive Scott is Professor Emeritus of European Literature at the University of East Anglia and a Fellow of the British Academy. His principal research interests lie in French and comparative poetics (*The Poetics of French Verse: Studies in Reading*, 1998; *Channel Crossings: French and English Poetry in Dialogue 1550-2000*, 2002 [awarded the R.H. Gapper Book Prize, 2004]); in literary translation, and in particular the experimental translation of poetry (*Literary Translation and the Rediscovery of Reading*, 2012; *Translating the Perception of Text: Literary Translation and Phenomenology*, 2012; and in photography's relationship with writing (*The Spoken Image: Photography and Language*, 1999; *Street Photography: From Atget to Cartier-Bresson*, 2007). Translation and photography combine in his recent *Translating Apollinaire* (University of Exeter Press, 2014). He is at present working on literary translation's broader connections with aesthetics, comparative literature, ecology and ethnography.

Acknowledgements

The editor and contributors would like to make the following acknowledgements:

Gillian Beer: thanks to the organizers of the international conference on W.G. Sebald held at UEA in 2008 for which this essay was first prepared.

Jon Cook: thanks to Dr. Barbara Cooke for help in preparing the manuscript and to the School of Literature Drama and Creative Writing and the Faculty of Arts and Humanities at YEA for their support.

John Coetzee: thanks to Random House.

Tacita Dean: 'W.G. Sebald' was first published as part of *Seven Books* to accompany Dean's exhibition at Musée d'Art Moderne de la Ville de Paris, May 7 - June 22, 2003. Published by Steidl, Germany.

Tess Jaray: 'A Mystery and a Confession' first appeared in Tess Jaray's collection *Painting: Mysteries and Confessions* published by Lenz Books (2010).

Robert Macfarlane: an earlier version of the essay in this volume first appeared in 2005 in *Zembla* magazine, edited by Dan Crowe. The author would like to thank Dan Crowe.

Will Self: thanks to Professor Amanda Hopkinson who, as the then Director of the British Centre for Literary Translation, commissioned an earlier version of this essay as the W.G. Sebald Memorial Lecture for 2010.

The photograph of W.G. Sebald on the back of the jacket is reproduced courtesy of UEA.

Every effort has been made to credit the copyright of texts and images reproduced in this book. Please contact the publishers regarding errors or omissions for correction in any subsequent editions of this collection.

First published in 2014 by Full Circle Editions
in association with the University of East Anglia

Introduction copyright © Jon Cook 2014

Essays in this collection copyright © The individual authors and
rights-holders: see acknowledgements and permissions on page 157

Artworks and photographs copyright © The individual artists and
rights-holders as acknowledged

The moral right of the authors and artists has been asserted

Design and Layout copyright © Full Circle Editions 2014
Parham House Barn, Brick Lane, Framlingham, Woodbridge, Suffolk IP13 9LQ
www.fullcircle-editions.co.uk

All rights reserved. No part of this work may be reproduced, stored
in a retrieval system or transmitted in any form or by any means without
prior permission in writing of the publisher. A CIP record for this book
is available from the British Library

Set in Miller & Gill Sans
Paper: Munken Pure 120gsm from FSC® Mix Credit

Book design: Jonathan Christie

Printed and bound in Suffolk by Healeys Print Group, Ipswich

ISBN 978-0-9571528-6-1

Note on the typeface:
Miller is a transitional serif typeface designed in 1997 by Matthew Carter
based on the "Scotch Roman" style which originates from types cut by
Richard Austin in Scottish type foundries in the early 19th century.